SINK & CONTAINER GARDENING

using dwarf hardy plants

First published 2001 by
Guild of Master Craftsman Publications Ltd
Castle Place, 166 High Street, Lewes, East Sussex BN7 1XU

ISBN 1 86108 200 2

A catalogue record for this book is available from the British Library.

Edited by Stephen Haynes
Designed by Fran Rawlinson
Cover design by Tim Mayer

Set in Adobe Garamond and Mrs Eaves

Colour origination by Viscan Graphics (Singapore)
Printed in Hong Kong by H&Y Printing Ltd

SINK & CONTAINER GARDENING

using dwarf hardy plants

Chris and Valerie Wheeler

GUILD OF MASTER CRAFTSMAN PUBLICATIONS

We would like to dedicate this book to our parents, for all their help,
encouragement and support over the years.

Contents

Introduction

This book takes a refreshing look at ways of creating and using all sorts of containers around the garden, from tiny pots and troughs to large half-barrels and sinks. Colour and interest can be created throughout the year using permanent plantings of a wide range of dwarf shrubs and conifers, perennials and grasses, alpines and bulbs. A careful selection of plants, even in one container, can create interest for much of the year, with one plant following on from another.

Many people with small, even tiny, gardens desperately want to grow plants. There is a real human need to have living, growing plants around us, to watch them throughout the seasons and to tend and nurture them. It can become an absorbing interest, whether you are young or old, at home all day or out at work. It is just as important if you are elderly or disabled, and containers can be raised in various ways to make them easier to tend. You can keep just a few containers outside the door or on the patio, or they can become an integral part of your whole garden.

Investing in more permanent plants for your containers, such as dwarf shrubs, small perennials and alpines, decreases daily maintenance by comparison with bedding plants. Hardy permanent plants don't need constant attention, and can last for several years without the expense of replanting every season.

Most gardens can be enhanced by the introduction of planted containers. Think of them as movable parts of the garden, used to enhance, to disguise and to cheer up. They are easy and quick to plant, requiring less overall maintenance than the ordinary garden, and can either create instant effect or develop during the seasons.

There is a huge choice of containers around, in many different materials – from genuine old stone sinks to home-made wooden troughs and from antique urns to stoneware and terracotta flowerpots, with a vast array in between.

We hope this book will encourage gardeners of all abilities to look afresh at the possibilities of sink and container gardening. Those relatively new to gardening will glean lots of practical information as well as planting suggestions. Seasoned gardeners will find inspiration and fresh ideas, using new or unusual plants and combinations to achieve striking effects. All will find that there are endless ways of enhancing a garden with planted containers.

OPPOSITE: Saponaria ocymoides *tumbles out of this terracotta chimney pot*

Why use sinks and containers?

There is a huge range of containers available to the gardener, in all sorts of sizes, shapes and materials, and to suit every budget. Each has its own advantages and its own particular character, and we will be discussing these in detail in Chapter 2. Here we examine the reasons for using sinks and containers in your garden.

Sinks and troughs

The types available include genuine stone sinks, and old porcelain sinks converted to make realistic imitations of stone ones. There are also several types of reconstituted stone sinks and troughs on the market.

IDEAL FOR LIMITED SPACE

Several sinks can be fitted into a small area, so they are ideal where space is limited. Their size makes them suitable for even the smallest garden, though they make equally attractive features for large gardens too.

Since little space is required to create an interesting feature, the small back gardens and even tinier front gardens of many modern houses can be full of interest. There may be no room for a border, but several plants in a sink can provide just as much colour and enjoyment.

The planting can consist of a selection of colourful alpines, chosen principally for their flowers, or any collection of plants that you find particularly appealing

This sink planted with a variety of alpines and surrounded by other plants shows what can be achieved in a limited area

or interesting. Alternatively, you can design a miniature landscape feature to mimic or portray a scene in small scale. These mini-gardens can be made permanent, given the right choice of plants, and will last many years with a little care and attention.

Growing plants in sinks allows a wide range or variety to be accommodated in a limited amount of space. You can grow miniature trees, shrubs, alpines and bulbs, so there is no restriction on the type of plant you can collect – you just need to scale down!

GARDENING AT A COMFORTABLE HEIGHT

Sinks are usually raised above ground level, allowing easier appreciation of the plants they contain. Tiny plants would simply be lost if planted in the general garden borders, overwhelmed by larger ones. In heavy soil, many smaller plants just would not have a chance of surviving anyway. Planted in raised sinks, together with others of similar scale, they have far more chance of thriving, of being noticed and appreciated. It is much easier to see and admire a small-scale plant when it is raised 30–45cm (12–18in) above ground level.

Raising the plants means less stooping to tend them, so sinks are also ideal for older or less able gardeners. It becomes more difficult to bend right down to ground level as you grow older, so being able to tend to plants at a decent height makes looking after them much easier and more enjoyable. Sinks can be placed on blocks, or even on a substantial pedestal to raise them higher still.

Many disabled people derive huge enjoyment from gardening. Physical disability need be no bar to the satisfaction of growing plants and watching them maturing, flowering, changing colour with the seasons. If plants are at a height where you can reach them easily, you may well be able to do all the necessary tasks without assistance. Sinks can be raised up on blocks to a comfortable height, and if they can be accessed from all sides, so much the better. Make sure they are completely stable. Wheelchair-bound gardeners can enjoy gardening in sinks without the strain and fatigue of having to bend down to work at ground level.

Although small-scale gardening in sinks requires less activity, it can still be an endless source of interest and an absorbing pastime. Plants, after all, still need

These sinks are raised above ground level, allowing their contents to be easily appreciated

watering, deadheading, pruning and tidying up, whatever their scale.

CUSTOMIZED SOIL MIXES

Soil mixes can be adapted to the plants' requirements, so a range of different environments can be created for particular groups of plants.

Many alpine plants are happiest in a well-drained, gritty soil, which can easily be achieved in a sink by mixing compost specially. A good general compost mixture will suit many plantings of miniature conifers, dwarf shrubs and alpines, and extra grit can be added for those requiring a very free-draining compost. The mixture can be adapted for lime-loving plants by adding limestone chippings, and for woodland-type plants by incorporating peat and leaf-mould. Lime-hating plants will thrive in special ericaceous compost, which is more acidic.

Composts are dealt with in more detail in Chapter 6, but you can see already that a wide variety of plants can be grown in composts mixed specifically to suit them. You are not restricted by the soil type available in your garden. In fact, you could grow plants of each type in different sinks right next to each other.

If you have room for just two or three sinks in a tiny garden, and you have both a sunny and a shady area, you can create various environments. You can grow sun-loving, colourful alpines in a sharply drained mix in one; tiny ferns, saxifrages and other shade-lovers in a more peaty compost in another; and small

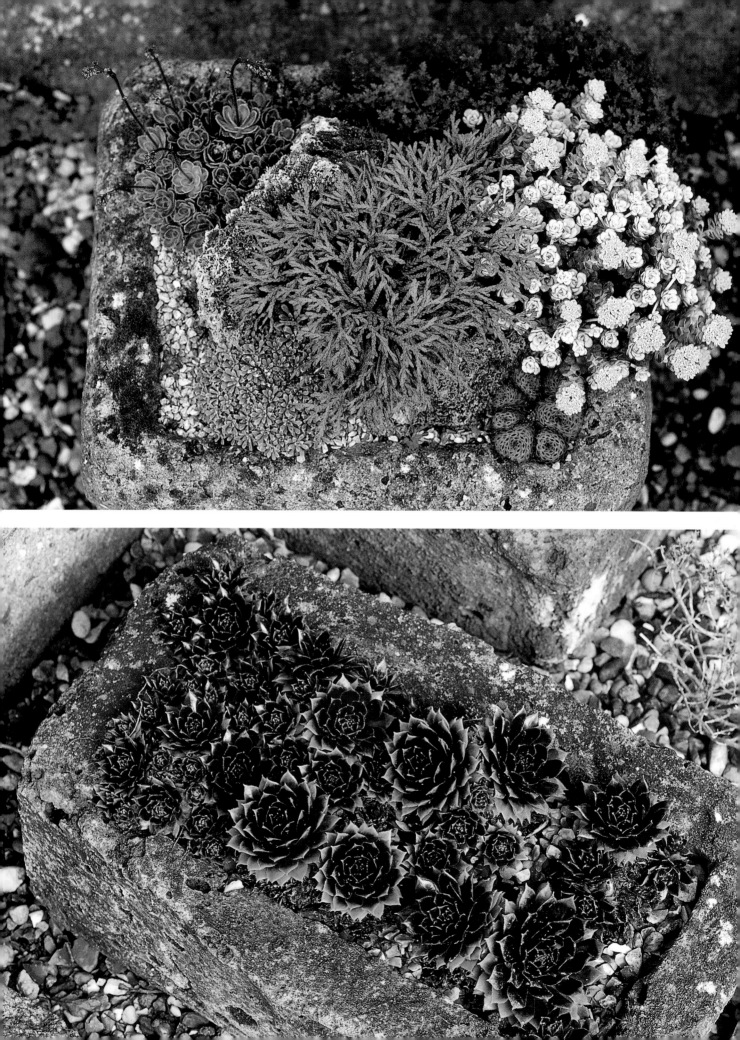

rhododendrons, cassiopes and similar ericaceous plants in the next. You can therefore have a whole spectrum of growing conditions – and the plants that thrive in them – in a very small space.

IDEAL FOR TINY ALPINES

Anyone who grows tiny alpines knows their magical appeal – the minute scale of the leaves and flowers has a special fascination. These plants would get totally lost if planted in an ordinary border; many would not even get noticed among the larger plants, which would easily swamp them, cutting off the light supply, so they would be unlikely to live very long. The soil could also be too heavy or coarse for them, with insufficient drainage. It is far better to grow these little plants in a sink with a soil mix they will be happy in, and where they can be seen, admired and enjoyed.

Small plants growing together complement one another, as all are of a similar scale, so the overall effect is aesthetically more pleasing.

IDEAL FOR THE ENTHUSIASTIC COLLECTOR

Sinks and troughs are ideal for growing particular collections of treasured alpines and other small plants. Many people have a passion for a specific type of plant, or a particular plant genus, and growing them in sinks allows them to be displayed together very effectively. It is important, of course, that all the plants in one sink have the same soil and light requirements, but otherwise there is no limit to the sort of collection that can be assembled.

Many people with an interest in alpines begin by growing a few sempervivums, or houseleeks. These succulent rosette-forming plants are available in a huge range of sizes and colours, and are one example of a plant that lends itself to collecting. They are very effective in a sink, especially when rosettes of varying

OPPOSITE ABOVE: *A tiny hypertufa sink (see page 11) with a perfectly proportioned selection of small-scale plants*

OPPOSITE BELOW: *This* Sempervivum *in a home-made hypertufa trough belongs to a keen collector, who has several varieties. A collection can be as small or as wide-ranging as you like*

colours are planted together. This sort of collection is also very suitable for children, as the plants require minimal care and attention to grow well.

Your particular interest may be in sempervivums, saxifrages or primulas; miniature conifers; dwarf bulbs; ferns; ericaceous plants; cushion alpines; silver alpines; alpines from a particular region of the world. All of these groups can be grown very successfully in sinks and troughs.

An extensive collection can be built up in a very small area, and this kind of feature can be just as valuable in larger gardens as in small ones.

MINIATURE LANDSCAPES

Miniature self-contained landscapes appeal to many and have a charm of their own. A real garden in miniature can be created, using slow-growing conifers and shrubs, alpines and tiny bulbs. All the structure of an ordinary garden, and the types of plants found there, are present, but on a much smaller scale. Many small plants are little replicas of their bigger relatives; others are tiny in habit anyway. You can really use your imagination here. Use these little plants to portray a garden setting in miniature, thinking of shapes and textures as well as colour. You must try and get the sense of proportion right – balance is important, as the whole scene is viewed at once.

Miniature conifers are ideal for providing structure, being evergreen, with interesting foliage and tree shapes. They can be trimmed and clipped, and their trunks add to the 'proper' tree look. Very small, slow-growing dwarf shrubs, either deciduous or evergreen, will also form a backbone to the rest of the planting, and these too can be pruned to shape. You can obtain tiny *Cotoneaster, Spiraea, Berberis, Hebe, Ilex, Santolina, Jasminum* and *Salix*. There are also tiny ericaceous shrubs, such as *Pimelea, Rhododendron, Andromeda* and *Cassiope*. Use little mound-forming hummocks and compact carpeters, with tiny grassy-looking plants. *Scleranthus biflorus* is a dense cushion plant with minute needle-like leaves and tiny flowers, which will form itself into realistic 'grassy' mounds and hummocks. Other small plants can grow up through the cushions, making a miniature mossy bank or grassy path. By sowing seeds of tiny alpines into *Scleranthus biflorus* you can make a very natural-looking feature. The silver *Raoulia* species also form spreading mats, climbing over stones and rocks or the edges of a sink to mimic their shape – though these are less fond of damp northern winters.

If you wish, you can embellish these scenes with gravel paths, tiny ponds and fences, but it depends on what exactly you want to achieve. Don't go overboard with embellishments – a perfectly lovely small landscape can be made using plants alone.

Other containers

All sorts of containers can be used for permanent planting, creating long-lasting, attractive features. These plantings add structure and interest to any garden, whatever its size.

Evergreen plants give permanent year-round structure and foliage, and can be supplemented by more seasonal plants such as bulbs and perennials, which add interest and colour at different times of the year. Deciduous shrubs in containers are more appealing during winter and early spring if they are surrounded at their base by small winter-flowering cyclamen and early bulbs; these will provide colour at a time when the shrub's branches are bare.

MOBILITY

Movable containers can be sited in full view or in a prominent position when the plants are at their best – in full flower, or with autumn leaf colour – then moved to a less conspicuous resting place when they are less attractive or have died down. Plantings consisting solely of bulbs or herbaceous perennials, for instance,

Snowdrops and cyclamen provide colour and interest around the base of a deciduous **Prunus** *in early spring*

A container planted with dwarf **Forsythia** *'Paulina' and narcissi looks wonderful in spring, and can be moved when the display is over*

A group of evergreen coloured foliage plants, including Ligustrum, Hebe, Santolina, Carex *and* Lamium, *disguises these bare walls*

will look very untidy and messy, not to say boring, when they are dying off or dormant. The container can be moved and left (continuing to water it when necessary) until the plants re-emerge the following year. Alternatively, the contents can be replanted elsewhere and the container potted up with a fresh arrangement. If you have several containers, you can arrange a succession of plantings to follow on from each other, so you continually have something to look forward to. Planning such displays adds greatly to the enjoyment of this form of gardening.

DISGUISING EYESORES

Essential but unattractive objects such as water butts, pipes and oil tanks can be partially disguised by strategically placed containers. Evergreen shrubs and long-flowering perennials are especially useful here;

choose those with large, bold foliage, flowing stems and a bushy habit to give a softened outline. Cheer up expanses of wall, fence, concrete and slabs by adding greenery or splashes of colour to these dull areas.

FILLING GAPS

Attractively planted pots can also be used to fill in gaps in borders after bulbs or annuals have finished. Clumps of bulbs always look forlorn once flowering is over, and you really need to let the leaves die away naturally, so put a planted container among them to draw the eye away and make the spot more interesting or colourful in the meantime.

This is one aspect of container gardening that is often overlooked, but it is a simple and very effective way of cheering up blank spots in the border at certain times of the year. As you walk round your garden, you

will come to recognize those areas that could do with a lift at particular times. You can have fun planning what to plant up to enhance those bare spots. If you have plants in position that will subsequently fill these blank areas – such as perennials springing into growth, or a shrub coming into full leaf – you can move your container to another spot when the time comes.

SUITING THE SOIL TO THE PLANT

We have already considered this topic in terms of sinks and troughs, but pots and other small containers give even more flexibility, allowing you to tailor the mix to the individual plant. Many people long to grow certain plants in their garden, but find they are unable to because the soil has too much lime in it, or is too sandy or too heavy, or the plant they hanker after is fussy as to its situation. It is amazing how everyone wants to grow the wrong sort of plant! However, this is where containers of all sorts come into their own.

Plants that you can't grow in the open garden because of soil type can be grown in pots with a compost mix that suits them. You can grow that particular *Rhododendron* or *Pieris* you really love in a finely textured, lime-free compost mixture. That silver filigree foliage plant that needs dry, sandy, well-drained soil can be grown even if you have solid, heavy clay, by giving it free-draining compost in a pot. Plants that resent too much moisture at their necks or roots can be provided with extra drainage in the form of crocks and open, free-draining compost. Plants that resent exposure are also happier in containers if these can be placed in more sheltered positions.

Bear in mind, though, that your garden's microclimate is also important. The amount of heat, rain, wind, etc. will have an impact on what you can successfully grow. For example, autumn gentians are much happier in damper conditions than in very dry areas, so even if you provide the required lime-free compost and water them using rainwater, they are not always successful in some locations. They are not happy in our own dry East Anglian climate, so we don't grow them, as we never get their full flowering glory. Conversely, plants that love arid conditions will suffer in very damp environments.

However, many of the problems involved in growing some plants can be overcome by using containers, and it is always worth experimenting with something you really want to grow.

OPPOSITE: *A stunning autumn show of colour from this* Acer *hides a large, bare expanse of fence*

2

Choosing sinks and containers

There is a huge range and variety of containers to choose from. They are available not only from garden centres and nurseries, but from hardware stores, the multiples, specialist potteries, markets, flower shows and reclamation yards. Alongside the more conventional pots, tubs and urns can be found more unusual containers that you may not have thought of using. It is always interesting to see how other people have adapted unusual containers. Visiting gardens which occasionally open to the public (as under the Gardens Scheme in Britain, or on 'open village' days) can be a wonderful source of inspiration and ideas.

Most containers are wider at the rim than at the base, but make sure the base is wide enough to be stable. Containers with narrow necks can look very attractive, but remember that it will be very difficult to remove plants once established, as the mass of roots and compost will be so much wider than the opening. This sort of pot is best used empty as part of a display, either upright or on its side. Some pots come with matching saucers; others have separate little pot feet to stand them on.

All containers used for plants need adequate drainage holes in the base, in sufficient number for the size of the container. If you are adapting some sort of receptacle to use for planting, make sure you provide drainage holes. Even with a layer of crocks in the base, any container without holes will get waterlogged in wet weather or as a result of over-watering. Put crocks over the hole to prevent compost blocking it.

Original stone sinks

If you can come by an original old stone sink or trough, these are perfect for alpine plantings. Unfortunately they are now both scarce and expensive so, unless you are lucky enough to own one already or to inherit one, the price is likely to be prohibitive. The advantage of reclaimed old items is that they are likely to be already weathered and to have acquired a patina of age, with irregular patches of green moss and greyish lichen producing a mottled surface.

Good sources of reclaimed items such as these include local auction rooms, farm sales, junkyards and reclamation yards. The *Yellow Pages* in Britain list salvage yards under the headings 'Architectural Antiques' and 'Salvage & Reclamation', and it is also worth looking up demolition companies, which may sell salvage materials too. Items in stock at any one time will vary, so give yourself plenty of time to browse and look round at these places. If you do find something you like, the yard may be able to deliver locally, although they may charge extra for this. Be aware that these stone sinks are extremely heavy.

Porcelain sinks

The deep, white-glazed porcelain sinks which used to be found in pantries and kitchens are often known as 'butler sinks'. Although they often command high prices nowadays, they can still be found, particularly if you know someone is removing an old one from a kitchen. They are often seen planted up as they are, but the shiny white glazed surface is rather incongruous in

The shiny white surface of this glazed sink may look incongruous in a garden setting. This example is also rather sparsely filled with compost and plants

This one is well filled with attractive alpines, and the hypertufa coating gives a more natural, harmonious look

a garden setting. They will look far more natural if coated in a mixture known as hypertufa, which will give a realistic imitation of a stone sink. Hypertufa is a mixture of peat, sand and cement, to which water is added to give a consistency suitable for plastering onto the sink's surface, a process explained in detail in Chapter 6. The inclusion of peat gives a more textured appearance than concrete on its own. The white shiny surface is concealed by the mixture, and the hypertufa will gradually weather over time, with mosses and lichens growing over it. Spreading yoghurt or liquid manure over the surface to encourage the growth of mosses and lichens can speed up this ageing process.

Porcelain sinks can be found in several different shapes and sizes, as well as the usual kitchen type. We have some tiny ones – only large enough to hold two or three plants – that originated in a school laboratory, as well as some very deep ones with a lip and some long, shallow ones. It is well worth asking round if you know of any houses or schools being renovated or cleared out, as many still have original porcelain sinks.

Home-made hypertufa sinks and troughs

Perfectly satisfactory sinks can be constructed at home, providing an inexpensive alternative to the real thing. The hypertufa mix of peat, sand and cement, instead of being applied over an existing structure, can be used with wooden, plastic or cardboard moulds to create a sink or trough shape from scratch. Again, this is explained in full detail in Chapter 6. Briefly, two moulds are required which fit each other with a gap of approximately 4cm (1$^{1}/_{2}$in) all round. The gap is filled with the hypertufa mix, which is left to set and harden. The retaining moulds are then removed.

This is a relatively easy 'fun' project, and the advantage is that you can create troughs of any size, in

This little home-made hypertufa trough has been constructed using cardboard moulds, leaving it with irregular rounded edges, and planted with an attractive Sempervivum

An old shower base, covered in hypertufa and planted with a selection of dwarf shrubs and alpines, is surrounded by a variety of plants in weathered terracotta pots

any roughly square or rectangular shape you wish – although large troughs are best reinforced with wire.

We have created several small troughs of various lengths and widths: square or long, squat or deep. We mostly use cardboard boxes for moulds, as these 'give' a little and create rounded edges, giving an irregular, slightly saggy and natural-looking result. Using wood as a base gives troughs of a very regular, angular shape with hard edges.

Reconstituted stone sinks

These range from relatively shallow sinks in different sizes for alpines, to deeper farmyard troughs and planters. Some manufacturers supply supports, made in the same material, to raise the sinks up. Reconstituted stone sinks can be a satisfactory substitute for original sinks, but you do need to hunt out the more realistic and natural-looking makes. The plainer ones are much to be preferred for alpine plantings. Very ornate, brightly or harshly coloured troughs are best avoided, as the charm of miniature plants will be overwhelmed by these. The more neutral-coloured they are, the better they will blend into your garden. Many have highly ornamental surfaces, with raised figures and flowers, which may appeal to some tastes, but troughs for alpine plantings are best kept as plain as possible. Any ornamentation is

more likely to detract from a miniature alpine planting than enhance it.

Reconstituted stone sinks do weather, but more slowly than natural stone. Treating with liquid fertilizer or yoghurt, as with hypertufa sinks, will encourage moss growth and give a more aged appearance.

Horse troughs and baths

Sometimes you might come across larger containers such as stone horse troughs, which in the right setting can make magnificent containers for alpines and dwarf shrubs. We have seen old cast-iron baths covered in hypertufa and planted up – but they still look like baths, and alpine plantings seem rather out of scale in them!

Terracotta pots

Traditional unglazed terracotta containers always harmonize well with plants and gardens, as their natural colour complements foliage and flowers so beautifully. It is worth searching out old terracotta flower pots, with their weatherworn surfaces and

OPPOSITE: *A varied selection of terracotta pots, including round, square and urn-shaped ones, some with relief moulding around the outside*

Terracotta pots are available in all sorts of different shapes and sizes

attractive. Trailing plants such as thymes are also effective in these.

Terracotta containers are porous, so they do need watering frequently. However, their porous nature means compost is less likely to become waterlogged or to overheat.

Terracotta pans or shallow bowls are excellent containers for alpines and other low-growing plants. Strawberry or herb pots have several holes in the sides, and these can be planted with a selection of herbs, or with rosettes of *Sempervivum* or *Lewisia*, which thrive because of the excellent drainage around individual plants. Multipots, in which three or more terracotta pots are fused together, look appealing but are not always practical, as they often lack drainage holes and each pot is rather small.

Wooden containers

These need to be treated with a preservative that will not harm the plants. Use products recommended for greenhouses – not creosote, which is harmful to plants. Wooden containers can be painted instead; there are lots of wood stains and washes available that have been developed for outside use. These can be very attractive in the right context.

sometimes irregular shapes. A huge range of new terracotta is produced by potteries, in all sorts of designs. You can find machine-made terracotta – which is cheaper – as well as the more expensive but more individual pots made by hand. New unglazed terracotta pots are best soaked in water before using, to moisten them and remove any salts from the clay.

The disadvantage of terracotta is that it may crack in frost. This is particularly true of older pots and certain types of new ones. If you are buying new, those fired at very high temperatures are more resistant to frost, so it is worth checking labels or asking suppliers for advice.

We have found that terracotta containers standing on hard surfaces, such as concrete or patio slabs, stand a better chance of surviving intact if raised off the surface on a piece of wood. This prevents the pot from freezing directly to the concrete or stone, making damage less likely. Placing susceptible containers in drier, more sheltered conditions is also advisable. Don't try to move frozen pots, though – leave them until thawed, or you are likely to crack or break them.

However, pots will get broken or cracked occasionally. If badly damaged, just use them as a source of crocks. Pots with a largish piece broken out of the rim can still be used – perhaps with small plants, more like a trough planting – and can look very

A small half-barrel imaginatively planted with Sempervivum *varieties cheers up an area of paving*

A colourful collection of alpines in a simple wooden planter

Wooden half-barrels are useful for large features; bear in mind that they are too big to move easily once planted up. They are ideal for larger shrub and perennial schemes, as several plants can be fitted in the one container. If you have enough room and somewhere suitable to place them, half-barrels do look very rustic; they are best with several trailing plants down the sides to soften them. You can char the interior (using a gas blowlamp with great care) to help reduce rotting. Barrels are best kept wet if not in use, as this swells the wood and prevents the staves separating. Make sure the metal bands are secure before you fill the barrel, whether it is a new or second-hand one.

Rustic tubs are smaller than barrels; they are made by some garden product manufacturers, and are available in garden centres and hardware stores. They can be found in various wood colours, such as oak and 'chocolate', so choose ones to complement your garden setting and existing plants. If you are planting alpines and dwarf shrubs in these, you can drill some holes in the sides for trailing or cushion plants, which will enhance the effect.

Wooden planters are available in all shapes and sizes, some of much better quality than others. You can also make your own wooden planters, which is ideal if you want one tailor-made for a particular spot. Some planters are constructed of half-round timber, fixed to corner posts and with a base and feet. They can be square or rectangular, or have more elaborate shapes, and can be of varying depths. They can also be tiered to give different levels of planting. Don't forget that the larger they are, the more difficult they will be to move once filled. Use smaller planters if you intend to shift them around frequently.

Window boxes

Wooden or plastic window boxes are available which are light enough to attach either above or below the sill. Wooden ones set off the plants much better because they look more natural, and can easily be stained. Wood also acts as an insulator against the cold in winter and the heat in summer. Highly coloured or ornamental window boxes are best avoided for permanent plantings, as they will clash and compete for attention with the plants. They can look effective with very simple plantings – for instance a single type of bulb – but otherwise boxes are best kept plain. Wooden boxes can be painted or stained, but aim for a natural, neutral effect. Some of the more subtle colours amongst the wood stains and washes available for outdoor use would look fine. Plastic window boxes are cheap and very lightweight, but find the sturdiest ones you can, as they will last longer.

Stone containers

Reconstituted stone planters and tubs are available from several manufacturers, and vary in quality and appearance. The colours range from a pale greyish stone to creamier shades. Many have surface ornamentation to give them the appearance of barrels or ornate urns; others have a brick effect, or are heavily scrolled, or decorated with leaves, flowers or figures. Choice of these is down to individual taste, but do try and pick containers that will blend into your garden and complement the plants you are going to use.

Decorated pots are more striking when planted with bold foliage than with lots of tiny, fussy plants or leaves. Both the plant and the container are then competing on equal terms, rather than the container completely overwhelming the plants.

Glazed earthenware pots and bowls

These have an unglazed interior, usually cream in colour, and a shiny, glazed exterior. They are available in several colours, of which muted greens, blues and browns are most attractive with plants of a distinctive or architectural character. For more brightly coloured pots, use simple, bold plants or groups. The low bowl shapes can be found in quite large sizes, which makes them excellent for alpine and *Sempervivum* displays, and for low, spreading plants.

Plastic containers

These are available in an enormous range of sizes, shapes and colours, and have the advantage of being light in weight as well as long-lasting and inexpensive. Compost will also tend to dry out less rapidly than in porous containers. Sturdy, heavy-duty plastic containers will last longer than very cheap ones, which tend to fade and become brittle. The most appropriate colours to use are black, green and terracotta. Although plastic pots are less aesthetically pleasing than some other materials, they are very useful for larger plants as they can be moved more easily. If arranged in a group, other pots and plants can more or less disguise a large plastic pot; alternatively, lush trailing plants can cover the sides. There are now some very realistic terracotta-coloured plastic containers, with slightly textured matt surfaces, far removed from the usual shiny ones, and these can fit in perfectly well with other types of pots.

Hanging baskets

Although usually planted for summer display with colourful annuals, there is no reason why you can't have a more permanent planting in a hanging basket. There are several types:

Wire baskets are usually plastic-coated and hung by a metal chain and hook. These need to be lined in some way, either with moss and plastic or with a basket liner made of compressed fibre, foam plastic or coconut fibre. Holes can be made in the plastic or liner for plants to grow through, giving greater coverage over the whole basket.

Plastic baskets do not need lining, and sometimes have a water reservoir or saucer attached. These may be hung by a plastic hanger or a chain and hook. You can't

This colourful hanging basket shows what can be achieved using alpines

Hypericum cerastioides *in a terracotta chimney pot*

achieve such lush plantings in these, as you can usually only plant in the top – though some have side holes, and in any case trailing plants will soften the effect.

Other types of **rustic basket** can be found – made of twigs, for example – which look particularly appropriate in country gardens.

Baskets, especially the larger and heavier ones, require a strong support to hold them – either a bracket or a large hook. They can be planted with small dwarf evergreen shrubs, bushy and trailing alpines, small perennials or herbs, with dwarf bulbs and pansies for seasonal colour.

Use a proportion of loam in the compost, but not too much or it will be too heavy. Keep well watered, and in winter choose a sheltered position away from draughts and drips. Top up with some fresh compost in spring, and replenish the outer moss if you are using this. Feed during the growing season, or add a long-term fertilizer each spring.

Chimney pots

Clay chimney pots can be obtained in a range of sizes and styles, mostly in terracotta, grey and stone colours. Original old ones are now scarcer and therefore more expensive, but can be found on demolition sites and in reclamation yards.

They are especially effective with trailing plants, and look good in groups of different heights, or placed among other plants in the gravel garden or border. As they are completely open at the base, fill with a good layer of crocks or gravel first – up to halfway in tall ones, to save on compost. Chimney pots can be plain or decorated, some having very attractive rims. They are relatively narrow, so are best for single plants or two or three smaller or trailing types.

You can also use large sections of drainpipe in the same way. These may be glazed or unglazed.

Logs

Large hollow logs make effective containers, as do hollowed-out tree stumps. Remove any rotting wood, clean back to solid wood, then char to prevent further rotting. Unusual old pieces of log can have smaller sections cut out to accommodate plants such as *Sempervivum, Sedum* or small bulbs. These require little soil, so will happily colonize pieces of log prepared in this way. Ivy is effective growing around logs, particularly if a group of logs is arranged together.

Large tree branches can be placed in suitable spots in the garden, singly or in groups, and the hollows planted up with suitable small plants. They look attractive in strategic spots at the front of a border surrounded by lush planting, or in a woodland area, at the edge of a gravel planting or the end of a path.

All sorts of containers can be put to use. These Sempervivum *plants have made themselves totally at home in a concrete block and a section of drainpipe*

3

Siting and grouping containers

Containers can be positioned almost anywhere in the garden, depending on the effect you want to achieve, the individual plants they have in them, and what sort of garden you have. Each container needs to be placed to suit the plants, in a position where it will enhance the surroundings and where you can appreciate and enjoy it. Remember that the advantage of a container is that it can be moved (if not too large and heavy), so if it doesn't look right after a while, you can always try it somewhere else.

This book is concerned with long-term plantings in containers, rather than bedding plants. The colours of many hardy plants tend to be comparatively subtle and muted, so it should be easy to find suitable sites where they fit in with existing plantings. This is not to say that you can't have exciting colour combinations and striking foliage – you certainly can, but the combinations are less likely to clash with other plants.

A weathered terracotta container of sweetly fragrant dwarf lilac, Syringa meyeri var. spontanea 'Palibin', creates a focal point outside a front door

Some ways to use planted containers

MAKING A STATEMENT

You may have a place in your garden where a stunning group of plants in a large container could create a focal point: against a bare wall of the house, for instance, or at the end of a path. Other good places to put a really special planted container are next to the front door, against a fence or hedge, or in any spot which can be viewed from a window.

You can make a statement either with a dramatic or showy plant or arrangement, or with a large, impressive container, planted in a way that does not detract from it. An ornate urn with a simple evergreen – such as clipped box, or a standard dwarf myrtle – always looks impressive, provided the plants are kept in excellent condition. A decorative glazed pot in either muted or bright colours could contain a bushy variegated *Euonymus*, a striking bronze sedge with arching foliage, or a rounded dwarf *Hebe* with evergreen foliage and

white or lilac flowers in season. More seasonal plants could include a pot full of dwarf iris, making a lovely display for a few weeks, or a large container of hellebores, which will give you weeks of purple, green or white flowers in early spring. A pot filled with *Anthemis* will provide attractive foliage as well as a long succession of daisy-like flowers over the summer; this would look stunning in a glazed blue or green pot.

Some dwarf shrubs are ideal for this purpose at their best time of year. Put them in a prominent position when they are looking wonderful, then move them and replace with something else when their display is over. The dwarf lilac *Syringa meyeri* var. *spontanea* 'Palibin' is stunning when in full flower, producing masses of flowers even on young plants. It will happily grow in a container for many years. Place it where you and your visitors can catch the glorious scent as well.

OPPOSITE: *An old terracotta pot with a standard rosemary adds height and interest among the plants in this border*

Similarly, *Prunus incisa* 'Kojo-no-mai', with its distinctive zigzag twigs, is smothered in pale pink flowers in spring, looking very attractive against a dark background. Small bulbs in white, cream, mauve or blue planted at its base would add to the effect and give you a longer-lasting display. With age, this small, bushy tree forms a low, rounded shape, and again could be kept for many years in a decent-sized pot. It has a further season of interest when the leaves take on orange and red tints before falling in autumn. Some autumn-flowering *Cyclamen hederifolium* around the base could enhance this. The zigzag twigs form an interesting pattern in winter, and you could add *Cyclamen coum* and snowdrops for winter and early spring colour.

This shallow pan of heathers makes a simple but effective display by a front door

ENHANCING AN AREA

Planted containers are, above all, the ideal solution to cheering up bare expanses of concrete or stone slabs, brick or wood. Every garden needs hard areas for paths, drives and patios, and fences and walls are required for division or screening. Many houses have bare areas of brick, stone or rendered wall. Vast expanses of patio or decking cry out for colour and softening foliage to be added, and this is where containers of all sorts come into their own. Plants in containers soften hard surfaces and integrate them with the rest of the garden.

They can be arranged on any hard surface, and against bare walls, fences and hedges. Arrangements of pots or single containers can be placed outside a door, around windows and near garden seating, instantly cheering up or enhancing these areas. You can enjoy them close up or from a distance.

FILLING GAPS LEFT BY SEASONAL PLANTS

Bulbs and herbaceous plants take up plenty of room in many borders, and are lovely from the time they first emerge, right through to leafing out and flowering. However, once they start dying away, they often look messy and rather unsightly. Large gaps become evident, which usually remain until the following season –

A selection of plants, chosen for spring colour, carefully arranged outside a door

unless you have planned your planting in layers so that new plants take over as others are fading. The alternative is to place a container in the gap, planted so as to harmonize or contrast with the plants around it.

Bulb foliage needs to be left to die down naturally – a process which often takes weeks – so you can't actually plant anything else in its place. However, you can put a pot (or more than one if there is room) among the fading leaves. Try and find gaps so that the container is sitting largely on the soil, rather than squashing all the bulb foliage. You could also raise the pot on those little pot feet that are available, or on pieces of brick, but make sure it is stable. However you arrange it, the plants in the container will be raised above the ground, thus drawing the eye up and away from the bulbs, and keeping the potted plants clear so they can be enjoyed. If you include some trailing plants as well, these will disguise the foliage of the bulbs even better.

The same applies to herbaceous perennials, although these tend to have a longer season of looking attractive. Many are best cut down in mid- to late summer, going on to produce a fresh crop of leaves for late summer or autumn, then dying down in late autumn or winter and remaining dormant or barely visible until spring. During the times when they are cut back or dormant, you can place planted containers around and among them, being careful not to squash them under the pot. The container planting will then provide the interest in that spot until the perennial begins to look good again. You can also use a planted container in areas left bare by annuals once they have been removed.

Of course, you don't have to fill every gap in a border. This approach works best where the gap is especially prominent – perhaps it is visible from a window or seat, or is in a spot passed by frequently.

Containers put among plants in the border also add extra height, which can be an advantage; and the pots themselves can be attractive additions among the foliage.

Trust your own judgement: experiment with different containers in various places to see the effect for yourself.

An impressive feature has been created using a number of sinks together, complemented by plants in the surrounding gravel

A large pan of colourful sempervivums sets off the corner of this border

MAKING THEM A FEATURE IN THEIR OWN RIGHT

In any garden there are bound to be places where a feature could be made of a planted pot or group of containers. The effect can be formal or informal, a small arrangement or a large collection. Think of a plain flight of steps, either leading up to a door or connecting different levels in the garden. These could be transformed by the addition of a row of pots, one on each step all down one side, planted with identical neat plants for a formal setting, or overflowing with informal plants for a cottagey look. The area just outside a front or back door is a prime spot for a beautifully planted tub or a carefully arranged collection of plants, where they will be seen by everyone coming and going.

Sinks and troughs always make an interesting feature, and if you have several they can form an impressive grouping. They can be laid out with plenty of space between, perhaps on paving or gravel, with small plants set in the ground around them to soften the whole area. This sort of arrangement allows a very long season of interest, as you can incorporate plants for year-round display both in and around the troughs. This can also be done, on a small or large scale, with other pots and containers of various sorts. The containers will look best if they have some common link or theme, rather than being in a wide variety of different materials and colours. Different-shaped pots which are similar in colour and type of material will always look more harmonious than a motley collection of black plastic pots, terracotta pots, shiny blue-glazed bowls and ornately scrolled reconstituted stone urns.

Always keep in mind the sort of style and effect you want to achieve, but don't be afraid to experiment. Pots are movable, so play around with an arrangement until it looks right to you. After all, you are the one who will be looking at it.

A FEW MORE IDEAS

- Try standing two or three pans of alpines on a small gravel area, perhaps where a paving stone has been removed, or at the corner of a small bed.
- An urn-shaped pot can look impressive standing by a decking area or next to a small pond.
- A pot with a striking foliage plant, or a colour-themed arrangement of plants, can be used to accentuate the end or corner of a bed.
- A single container can be a stunning centrepiece.
- Massed containers can create a colourful and interesting spectacle. A mass of small pots, tumbling over with plants, looks at home in a country-style or cottage garden. In a more formal setting, restrained plantings in large, elegant pots would be more in keeping.

A tumbling mass of informally planted pots is ideal for a country garden. Here, Dianthus, Gypsophila *and* Campanula *make a colourful display beside a conifer*

This large half-barrel was put in place before filling, as the final weight would make it very difficult to move. The planting of Sempervivum *and the carefully arranged terracotta pots make a feature in front of the* Ceanothus *bush*

Siting containers

POINTS TO CONSIDER

Although one of the reasons for having containers is that they are movable, there are some that it will obviously be impractical to keep shifting around, because of their size or weight.

Heavy containers and sinks will need to be moved into place before filling. This includes large half-barrels and tubs, large concrete or stone sinks, and any container that is likely to be too weighty to move once it is filled with compost and plants. Don't forget the extra weight once the container has been watered.

In all these instances you need to consider their position more carefully beforehand, as once the containers are filled it will be difficult to move them without emptying them. Make sure they are stable before you fill them, particularly if they are raised up on bricks or blocks.

Lighter and smaller containers can be moved around more easily, so use these for changing displays and temporary placements. If you are unable to move heavier materials, plastic pots which look like terracotta are ideal: they are considerably lighter than ceramic, terracotta or stoneware ones, even when full. Remember that the more permanent plants need compost containing a proportion of loam, and grit for extra drainage in some cases; this will make them heavier than displays of bedding plants, which are normally in peat-based compost only.

Make sure you don't obstruct well-used paths and walkways by siting pots awkwardly or without due consideration. The last thing you need is an obstacle

A whole array of terracotta pots, pans, chimney pots and sinks lines the path to the greenhouse — note that the pathway is not obstructed, leaving plenty of room to walk

course to get round the garden, which could be particularly dangerous for the elderly or infirm.

It is important to site containers according to the needs of the plants they hold. They may require full sun, partial or dappled shade, or full shade. It is no good having a shady spot and siting a pot of herbs or *Dianthus* in it to cheer it up, when these plants need full sun to thrive. This may sound obvious, but from experience we know that people do this sort of thing. Research the needs of your plants, if need be, to make sure you are giving them the conditions they will be happiest in. Read the label on the plant before you buy it, or ask the nurseryman, or look it up in a suitable book. If you are putting several plants in one container, make sure they need similar conditions to each other, including similar compost. It is perfectly possible to devise container plantings for all sorts of situations, as

long as the plants are suited. If you are not sure where to start, or just need some inspiration, you will find plenty of suggestions in Chapters 4 and 5 which you will be able to follow or adapt.

Containers can be moved to suit the changing requirements of the plants at different times of year. Some plants – particularly very early-flowering plants such as saxifrages and primulas – need as much light and sun as possible early in the year, but are happier in summer if placed in the shade, out of the full glare of the sun. They can therefore be brought out into full view, in prominent positions, when looking their best, and tucked away in a shady corner when flowering is over.

It is also important to consider the effects of the surrounding plants. Falling leaves from nearby bushes and trees in autumn can quickly smother small plants, so make sure that sinks, pans and small pots are not placed where this might happen. Plants clothed in foliage in summer may protect a container planting from wind and draughts, only to expose it once the leaves fall, so you may need to move that container if the plants in it are likely to suffer. Permanent plantings in hanging baskets are always best removed to a more sheltered position over the winter. If you have baskets planted up for winter and early spring display, check that they are hung out of draughts and strong winds, and away from drips. Wind scorch can be particularly devastating on some evergreen shrubs, as well as on softer foliage.

Think about your objective when siting containers: what exactly do you want to achieve?

~ To create impact or brighten up an expanse of patio, wall or decking, you may need several pots or a group of containers.

~ To provide a splash of colour in spring just outside your door, perhaps a simple pot of bulbs will suffice, or a mixed planting of a dwarf evergreen shrub, bulbs and primulas.

OPPOSITE: *This pan of saxifrages needs light for its early-flowering display, but must then be moved to a shady position for the summer*

A colourful pan of primulas brightens up a spot in front of a variegated Buxus

~ To grow a collection of plants for their own sake, you will not be so concerned about the containers; but even so, try and match them to the appearance of the plants so that they set them off well.

~ You may opt for a formal or informal display, one that blends in quietly or one that makes a dramatic statement.

SOME SAMPLE IDEAS

You will want to have spring bulbs on view when they are in flower, so place pots of them near the house or in places where they can be viewed from windows. They can then be removed when they have finished flowering. The same applies to containers with a mixture of bulbs and other plants; the shrubs or perennials included in these will conceal the bulb foliage somewhat as it dies down. Bulbs are always

cheering after the dull winter days, and it lifts the spirits to see them emerging and then flowering in succession. It is well worth the effort of planting dry bulbs in autumn or pots of growing bulbs in spring; they can be planted in groups on their own, used to underplant shrubs in pots, or mixed with other plants.

Early-flowering plants are best placed where they can be viewed from windows or paths, or outside a door – particularly as you may not want to venture to the farther parts of the garden at that time of year. Pans of *Saxifraga* in flower during the winter months give a long period of colour and interest, and can be grouped with pots of bulbs, hardy winter cyclamen and *Helleborus niger*. All these can be appreciated in a prominent position when they are at their best, and then moved somewhere else for the rest of the year.

Fragrant and aromatic plants are ideal in containers near seats, under windows, outside doors, alongside paths and on patios. In fact, they are excellent anywhere they can be brushed against or their perfume appreciated. They can be particularly enjoyed around seating areas in the evening, when their scent is often stronger. There are many suitable plants to choose from, including lavender, herbs, dwarf hyssop, *Artemisia* and pinks. These all enjoy the same well-drained compost and a spot in full sun, so you can either grow them in individual pots or group some together in a larger container.

Culinary herbs can be planted in a container close to the house – ideally outside the kitchen door or window, or within easy reach of steps or a path. You don't want to be wandering halfway down the garden just to pick some thyme or parsley at the last minute for your dinner. Use groups of herbs, making sure you plant together those that like the same conditions. Some may be better in individual pots, particularly those like mint that would smother everything else. Parsley is best on its own, too, as it requires a lot more water. Herbs also look attractive as a collection in a group of pots on or near your patio, outside a door, or in a herb pot or herb wheel.

A colourful foliage or flowering plant in season can be placed in front of a dull hedge or shrub. This is an ideal spot placement, especially useful near early-flowering shrubs that are usually duller during the summer months, or dark evergreen shrubs that act mainly as screening or background.

Identical formal plantings either side of a door look very smart in the right surroundings – at the front of a town house or a stylish modern house, for example – but would be out of place by a cottage or in an informal setting. Here, an asymmetrical, informal planting would look better, or a simpler planting on one side only, using one or more pots.

Grouping containers

A group of containers can make a stunning display, using various sizes of pot and contrasting shapes and colours of plants. What matters most is the effect you want to achieve, and what you find pleasing. Particular

arrangements recommended in design books can be used as a rough guide, but there is no need to follow them slavishly. However, ideas and suggestions are always useful, so here we present a few to get you started.

Containers usually look better when deliberately grouped rather than merely scattered about, particularly on a patio or an expanse of stone or gravel. A group is more visually attractive when arranged so that both containers and plants harmonize or contrast with each other – rather than a random dotting about of unlinked pots and a whole array of different plants. Some of the pots need to share a common theme: they could be similar in colour or shape, or some of them could have the same plants.

A grouping of pots of the same design, but in different sizes and shapes, always looks attractive, as

This informal grouping of pots shows variation in size and shape, but the terracotta colour theme gives a harmonious effect

there is immediately a common linking thread between them. You could have a large stoneware flowerpot at the back, flanked by two or three smaller ones of the same shape, and in the front a low pan and a short, rounded pot with handles. A collection of one pot, a low bowl and an urn-shaped container, all in terracotta, is another attractive possibility. This sort of group is very effective when the plants themselves harmonize. In a large grouping, try and have the same plant in two or three of the pots – particularly if you have several plants per pot – to give a common theme throughout. You could have the same trailing plant at the edge of some of the containers, or a clump of the same perennial, or a splash of bright colour from similar bulbs, primulas or pansies.

The same principles apply to using a group of containers that are not identical in design, but are similar in colour or texture. Again it is more effective to group different shapes and sizes together so that the plants are shown to better effect, with low bowls or pans at the front, graduating up to larger pots at the back. These arrangements do not have to be symmetrical, and in fact a more informal arrangement often looks much better – unless you feel a formal structure is more appropriate for a particular spot.

Some of the subtly patterned and textured pots and urns available are wonderfully suited to this kind of grouping, mixing well with more natural-coloured stoneware and terracotta pots. Those patterned with brown, muted or dark green, soft blue or brick red can look most effective.

A collection of pans or low bowl-shaped containers makes an interesting display, particularly with small bulbs, alpines or sempervivums; place these in a position where you can look down on them, as there won't be much height overall. If you have a collection of a specific type of plant, then grouping them together like this is an effective way of displaying them.

A harmonious collection of plants can look stunning in either similar or contrasting containers; in this case the plants themselves are the common link. It still helps if the containers look good together, and you don't use too many wildly clashing colours and materials. Make sure the containers don't detract too much from the plants. Brightly coloured pots can swamp plants with delicate foliage or pastel flowers,

*A display of **Sempervivum** varieties in individual terracotta pans is all the more effective when massed together like this*

but can look amazing with large, bold leaves or hot colours. Deep blue is a wonderful foil for white flowers, and dark green sets off golden colours beautifully or makes a good contrast to orange flowers. We are not keen on brightly coloured containers or white ones, but if you want to use these, choose your plants carefully.

A mixture of different containers will need more careful arrangement, perhaps using trailing plants to cover some of the surfaces and sides. Strategic positioning of pots or other plants can help to disguise any containers that you really don't like or don't want to show. If you have a large shrub in a big plastic pot, this can be well hidden by placing smaller, more attractive containers around it, so you still have the benefit of the plant but don't have to look at the black plastic.

If, like us, you tend to have groups of containers in spots that you frequently walk past – just outside the back door, for instance – you will want to have something fresh and new to look at most of the time. You could opt for one or more established container plantings that can be livened up at their duller times by adding pots or pans of colourful flowers or foliage at different times of the year. As these pass their peak or die down, they can be replaced by something else, so your group is continually changing throughout the year. Unlike bedding plants, you needn't discard your planted pots once their main display is over, but can just keep them until their next season if you wish. Containers with several plants in are invaluable as well: you can have a changing display for much of the year, all in one pot. However, these too can be used as part of a larger group of pots, with one or two seasonal displays added as you feel like it.

This may sound as though you will be swapping pots over continually, but in reality hardy plants have a long season of interest, and you will have weeks or months of display from most of them. Shrubs can remain where they are all year, forming a background to other container plantings, and most perennials are interesting to watch from the moment they emerge above soil level, unfolding their leaves, as well as bearing flowers. Don't get obsessed with removing pots as soon as one plant starts to die back, or some leaves begin to look rather bedraggled. Just tidy up any messy bits, and replace pots that are totally uninteresting once finished.

This group of perennials chosen for their contrasting foliage shows how leaves of varying shapes and colours can complement each other. The Hosta, Heuchera *and* Ophiopogon *are perfectly at home in this partially shaded setting*

A good place to display groups of containers is around seating areas in your garden, or on the patio, during the seasons when you are spending more time outside. A display of aromatic or colourful plants in these areas is ideal if you are likely to be relaxing or dining in the garden in summer. Fragrant plants are often at their best in the evening, so group these near seats or paths where you can brush against them to release their fragrance. Pots of lavender, rosemary, thyme, myrtle and other herbs look wonderful together, with their aromatic foliage and mostly muted, harmonious flower colours. These plants are well suited to pot culture, as they can be given the well-drained compost they prefer. A group consisting of standard rosemary, dwarf myrtle, one or two different lavenders, a bowl of lemon-scented thymes, a pan of golden *Origanum* and a silver *Artemisia* will look stunning for several months.

Many perennials have their peak flowering time in the height of summer, so grow some in containers and add them to groups of established plants in pots, or place a collection on your patio or in a blank spot in the border to cheer it up. Put them in place as the mounds of leaves start to look attractive, watch the buds emerge and then enjoy weeks of flowering. Deadhead regularly to encourage them to keep producing flowers, and you will have a display to be proud of. You can also add pots of summer-flowering bulbs, such as lilies or alliums.

Another way of grouping containers is to use a mixture of contrasting foliage shapes and colours, arranged so as to show each at its best. Many plants have interesting foliage that can be enjoyed even when they are not in flower, and this can be enhanced by contrast with different foliage types. Spiky, upright leaves can be set off by rounded, bun-shaped plants and trailing leafy stems. Mix upright, prostrate and hummock shapes, or put a cone-shaped conifer with a small bushy shrub. Clipped shapes can also be incorporated into container groupings, where they will contrast with leafy, flowing plants.

Large stones or pebbles can be an effective addition to grouped container settings. They can be used at the side or in front of a group, and are best used in quantities of three or more to make an impact.

You will find more development of these ideas, with suggestions for which plants to use in particular situations, in Chapter 4.

A newly planted group of sinks on a gravel area, allowing several plants to be grown in a small space. Log sections in the gravel serve as stepping stones, allowing easy access around the sinks

GROUPING SINKS

A grouping of sinks or troughs makes a wonderful feature in any garden, small or large. Depending on the area available, you could have a group of two or three small sinks, or a whole collection arranged together as part of a larger feature. Any grouping of sinks can accommodate a wide array of alpines and miniature shrubs in a relatively small space, and is a good choice even where space is not limited. A collection of sink plantings is endlessly fascinating, as there is always something new emerging or flowering.

You can group your sinks either on a hard surface, such as paving, or on a gravel area, where you can incorporate small plants around the sinks. Even on a paved area, there may be gaps or cracks in which you can plant other alpines, thereby softening the area around the sinks. Placing some trailing plants in the sinks to hang down over the sides will also reduce the amount of hard surface visible.

Standing your sinks on a gravel garden makes a very attractive feature. You can plant around and between the sinks, with some taller plants being placed to cover the sides, in addition to trailing plants within the sinks themselves. A diverse planting scheme including small grasses, bushy and shrubby alpines, and carpeting plants will give you a good mix of heights and textures. Make sure you don't have too many plants that are taller than the sinks, or they will look out of scale. In a large area, you can add stepping stones to make it easier to get round the gravel garden, and to break up the surface more.

Aim to plant a variety of shapes and colours in your sinks, to give you interest for much of the year. Some evergreens will provide all-year structure and foliage. Remember to choose plants suited to your conditions.

Small bulbs planted in the gravel at the base of this sink add interest to the whole area

Sinks are best placed in a permanent site, as they are extremely heavy, especially when filled. Decide where you want them before filling, and take especial care when moving hypertufa sinks as they can chip easily if knocked. You also need to ensure that you can reach all round them easily to tend the plants, so leave sufficient room between them.

These ideas for planning the siting and planting of your containers are discussed in further detail in Chapter 5. There you will find specific ideas for planting schemes, as well as suggestions on choosing your plants.

4

Plant selection

Many types of hardy plants are suitable for container growing. The types of plant we are discussing in this book include dwarf shrubs and conifers, perennials, alpines, grasses and sedges, herbs and bulbs. Any of these can be planted in containers individually, with others of the same kind, or in mixed groups.

Any planting which is intended to be permanent should contain fully hardy plants, so that the container does not need to be moved under cover for winter, nor wrapped up in fleece or sacks to protect it from the frost. If you have a greenhouse that you keep frost-free over winter, and you want to grow non-hardy plants, these can of course be grouped with other containers successfully during the summer. However, in this book we are concerned specifically with hardy plants that can be left outside all year

Dwarf shrubs and conifers

Although many shrubs and conifers can be grown in containers, we are concerned here with the smaller forms, reaching 90–120cm (3–4ft) or so, which can be kept in pots for many years, and which associate well with the other small plants discussed. There are many attractive dwarf shrubs available, and they are becoming increasingly popular because so many people today have smaller gardens and require plants in scale with them. These are perfect for pots and other containers, as their small size makes them very manageable; as they don't need huge containers to grow in, they can be moved around fairly easily. Being naturally compact, they are not inclined to get out of hand and rapidly swamp surrounding plants. Dwarf conifers are also valuable, as larger ones can quickly outgrow a container and become extremely pot-bound.

Shrubs and conifers play an important role in container gardening, as they provide structure and substance in any planting. They can add height or bulk to a group, and provide a framework of branches all year – and year-round foliage, if evergreen.

Conifers and evergreen shrubs are attractive all year, providing a background to smaller plants around them. Choose upright-growing forms to provide height, or prostrate forms if you want a solid, low backdrop for other plants. This doesn't mean they are boring, and merely there to set off their neighbours; evergreens can contribute a great deal to the overall effect. Look for evergreen shrubs with interesting or unusual leaves, and consider the textures and colours as well as the shapes. Flowering forms are even more of a bonus, as their flowers can give an extra dimension to the planting.

There are several excellent choices that can be grown in small pots or used to form low mounds in a more extensive planting. *Gaultheria procumbens* grows into a very low bush with attractive glossy green leaves covering its stems, and bears bright red berries. It requires lime-free compost, and is excellent in a wide, low pan or pot. Dwarf hebes, including prostrate forms, provide a range of foliage colour, from dark to pale green, yellow-green, grey, gold, purple or red-tinged. Many also have flower spikes in shades of mauve, pink or white, borne between mid-spring and late autumn, depending on the variety. One or other can be found to fit into most colour schemes. Dwarf box (*Buxus*) is dense and compact, and can be clipped to shape if desired. Sphere shapes are excellent mixed with other tidy plants; taller conical or spiral forms can add an interesting dimension.

More substantial shrubs can form a backdrop to a planting, or can be used in a large pot, either placed by itself or grouped with other pots. These shrubs can be used to form important structural effects, or simply to add bulk to a planting. They can provide different colours and textures with their leaves – use glossy or matt, rough-textured or smooth, plain or variegated

OPPOSITE: *The evergreen shrub* Mahonia aquifolium *looks impressive in spring with white* Helleborus niger *and a double indigo primrose, making a bright show in front of a more sombre shrub*

foliage, and think also about the effect and timing of any flowers they may produce.

The many named forms of *Euonymus fortunei* are valuable, being low shrubs that can either trail or climb through other plants. You will find varieties with green or variegated foliage, with differing proportions of either white or yellow; some are almost totally golden. All are outstanding for container use, associating brilliantly with all sorts of other plants. There are some dwarf bushy forms with dense foliage, also very suitable for pots.

Mahonia aquifolium and its named forms have shiny, leathery leaves and clusters of bright yellow flowers in early to mid-spring. Although normally grown as ground-cover shrubs, they can look impressive in a largish pot with other small, colourful plants.

Dwarf conifers are also excellent evergreens to use in container plantings, and forms can be found with dark or light green, blue or silvery, yellowish-green or golden foliage. Some have yellow tips or flecks, and their different shapes add interest, with columnar or bun-shaped forms, low spreading or rounded varieties. Upright shapes are good for adding height to a planting, while prostrate forms are invaluable for planting at the side of a pot.

Conifers are often seen on their own in pots, or with spring bulbs, but try associating them with small perennials and alpines to add colour and foliage. Purple and yellow look stunning with dark green conifers, giving an immediate lift to the sombre, deep colour. Try alpine campanulas and golden thyme. Blue

Miniature conifers add structure to the alpine plantings in these little hypertufa troughs

conifers form an excellent foil for white flowers, or you could try using plants with soft mauve and pink flowers, or a contrasting silver foliage plant.

Miniature conifers can be used in sink and trough plantings, but do make sure they are very slow-growing forms, as you want them to stay in scale for many years. Don't just choose ones *labelled* as dwarf, but research them carefully first and purchase from a specialist conifer or alpine nursery. There are different-shaped forms to choose from, with columnar ones adding height, prostrate ones to grow near the edge or over a rock, and bun-shaped ones to form little mounds.

Deciduous shrubs can be valuable for much of the year. Even without their foliage in winter, the shape and form of the branches and the tracery of twigs can create an interesting framework; and there are shrubs with coloured twigs which come into their own in the winter months. Deciduous shrubs often have bright new spring growth, either light, fresh green or pink- or red-tinted. Unfolding leaves bring spring interest, and in some shrubs flowers are borne before or at the same time as the new leaves.

One of the earliest to flower is *Forsythia*, and there are some small, compact forms suitable for container growing, including *F.* 'Paulina' which looks lovely and cheerful surrounded by dwarf narcissi. It is not overly interesting for the rest of the year, though, so bring it into a prominent position for the early weeks of spring and enjoy it by itself, or put later-flowering plants around it to follow on. Small forms of *Prunus* are a joy in spring, their flowers opening before or together with the new leaves. Some willows make interesting container plants; choose the smaller kinds, in either upright or prostrate forms, which will reward you with fluffy catkins in early to mid-spring.

Deciduous *Berberis* are available in a number of small forms, many with reddish-purple leaves, others with fresh green or golden foliage. These have yellow or golden flowers in mid-spring, the flower buds forming as the leaves start to emerge. *Berberis thunbergii* 'Erecta' is a fine, narrow upright shape, ideal for the back of a container, while 'Dart's Red Lady' is a bushy, spreading form with deepest red leaves. These varieties usually also have brilliant autumn foliage colour, extending their period of interest.

Autumn colour is another important feature to consider. Many deciduous shrubs take on yellow, orange, red or crimson tints before the leaves fall, and these can look very effective combined with late-flowering small perennials and alpines, or grasses with their bleached flower heads.

Many deciduous shrubs, of course, are grown for their flowers, some coming into bloom in early spring before the foliage develops, others flowering during the summer or early autumn. If you have a spectacular flowering shrub in a container, it is best if other plants around it aren't competing with or detracting from it, so choose foliage plants or ones that flower earlier or later, to spread the season. Less spectacular flowering shrubs can be complemented by plants that harmonize or contrast with them. For instance, the deep red leaves and numerous but small yellow flowers of *Berberis thunbergii* 'Dart's Red Lady' will be set off particularly well by silver foliage and mauve flowers, which will enhance rather than detract from the shrub. *Prunus incisa* 'Kojo-no-mai', on the other hand, which is a mass of pale pink bloom in early spring, looks best with no competition so that it can be fully enjoyed on its own; though you could underplant with snowdrops to flower beforehand, and hardy cyclamen to follow in the autumn.

Think of the shape and size of flowers as well as the colour; plants which are used together should be kept in some sort of scale with each other. Those with large flowers, such as *Hydrangea paniculata* with its conical flower heads made up of many tiny flowers and florets, need bold foliage plants to go with them.

Choose the shapes and growth habit of your shrubs so that they complement each other, or the other plants you put with them. If you are using three dwarf shrubs in a container (or in three individual pots placed as a group), don't use three bun-shaped plants or three upright ones. Instead, choose contrasting shapes that will enhance and draw attention to each other. A columnar shape, a rounded form and a prostrate form always look right together; a taller, bushy form, a dense, rounded shorter bush and a trailing shrub will also go together well. You can combine plants of similar shape, provided they contrast with one another in height or scale.

Many deciduous dwarf shrubs take on spectacular autumn leaf colour: this Zelkova serrata *'Goblin' in an earthenware pot is stunning with its green, gold and orange coloration*

Foliage and flower colours can be chosen to contrast or to harmonize. For example, use silver and red foliage together, or bright green with variegated yellow and green, or blue-green with variegated white and green. Purple and blue-grey go well together, as do blue-grey and silver. Soft green associates with most colours, red and purple add dramatic or deeper tones, and silver lightens any scheme.

If you are planting an individual shrub or conifer in a container, it is best to choose one which provides interest for much of the year – especially if you are using it completely on its own. If you can add other plants to complement the shrub at the times when it is not at its

A containerized **Euonymus fortunei** *'Golden Pillar' is lifted in spring with* **Narcissus** *'February Gold' and sulphur-yellow primroses, the golden theme harmonizing with the weathered earthenware pot against a red brick wall*

best, so much the better. These can either be put in the same container or grouped around it in pots of their own. The ideal shrubs to use as specimen plants are evergreens, or those which have a long flowering season or coloured foliage. Best of all are plants which can provide various points of interest at different seasons.

For example, a shrub might have coloured new growth in spring, be floriferous over a long period in spring or summer, then have autumn colour, followed by coloured twigs or an interesting framework in winter.

To find all these features in one plant would be a tall order indeed, but some shrubs can meet two or three of these criteria. Deciduous *Berberis* have coloured leaves, flowers and brilliant autumn tints. *Prunus incisa* 'Kojo-no-mai' flowers very profusely, with a long spring flowering season, and has autumn colour in its foliage and zigzag twigs that show up well in winter. *Cornus stolonifera* 'Kelseyi' (or 'Kelsey's Dwarf') has red and yellow twigs for winter and red-tinted foliage in autumn.

Alternatively, use a specimen shrub to create interest in a particular spot while it is at its peak, then move it to a less prominent position when past its best. You could use it as part of a group to add height, bulk or a framework. A simple shrub or conifer on its own deserves a special pot, but make sure it doesn't clash with any flowers.

Grasses and sedges

There are numerous types of grasses and grass-like plants that can be used to give shape, texture and colour contrast to a group. The foliage is typically linear, and finer in outline than most other leaves. It is usually upright or arching, forming slim columns, dense mounds or vase shapes. Grasses form a useful contrast to more solid plants with large leaves or bulky shapes, or to those with rounded foliage or tiny leaves. Slim, upright grasses contrast with mounded plants or trailers, while arching types go well with large-leafed shrubs or perennials, upright plants, or those with tall flowering stems.

Many grasses have a light and graceful presence, the fine leaves waving in the slightest breeze and the delicate flower heads in summer and autumn fluttering gently atop slender stems. Because you can often see through their light, narrow foliage, grasses lend an airy feel to a planting scheme and can lighten the bulk of other foliage. This is especially true when they are backlit, with the sun behind them. Sedges tend to have broader leaves, but they are still relatively narrow; they usually form low clumps or taller arching shapes, which give an added contrast in texture. In general, grasses require well-drained compost, whereas sedges need more moisture-retentive compost.

Grasses and sedges can be used in mixed plantings, with shrubs, conifers, perennials, alpines and bulbs, or with other grasses or sedges of contrasting form and

colour. They can also make excellent specimen plants, particularly those that are attractive all year round and don't need cutting down in spring. The bronze form of *Carex comans*, for instance, is probably best in its own pot; it will require a fairly large pot eventually, as the clump spreads by suckering slowly, forming a wonderful arching mound of bronze. A tall pot is ideal, or a pot raised up on a step or wall, so that the long, slender drooping stems with their little brown flowers can hang down and not drag on the ground. Just give it a haircut in late autumn to tidy the ends and old flower heads, and you can enjoy it all winter as well.

A grouping of three or five contrasting varieties of fescue (*Festuca*) will look attractive. Try *F. amethystina*, with very slender dark green leaves and violet flower heads nodding above them, together with *F. glauca* 'Elijah Blue', a shorter, silvery-blue tufted grass, and *F. eskia*, a very short, fine-leafed, bright green mound which takes on reddish tints in cold weather. Although the leaves of all three varieties are similar in form, interest is maintained by the varying heights of these grasses and the contrasting colours of foliage and flowers. You could also use individual grasses in pots as part of a group. They are wonderful with hostas, heucheras or tiarellas, providing contrast in foliage; but the grasses need better drainage than these plants, so are better in separate pots.

You will find grasses and sedges in a great variety of foliage colours, including striped or variegated types. There are many shades of green, from dark to light, as well as yellowish-green, golden, blue, silvery-blue and bronze. Some have leaves striped with yellow, gold, cream or white, either in a band down the centre of the leaf or as edging bands or narrow margins.

Blue and silver forms, usually *Festuca* varieties, are excellent with silver foliage plants, and with pastel or white flower schemes. They enjoy the same good drainage as most silver plants, and associate with other sun-lovers such as lavender, *Cistus* and *Helianthemum*. Bronze forms go well with golden foliage or flowers, or with contrasting soft green leaves. Golden forms look stunning next to deep purple or red foliage, or with purple, deep blue or sky-blue flowers. Striped leaves stand out best against solid colours, rather than mixing with other variegated foliage.

Most grasses are at their best in sunny positions, but some sedges are suitable for shady areas, so collectively they are extremely valuable for use in groups or plantings all round the garden.

Perennials

Herbaceous perennials are invaluable in permanent container plantings; they provide a wealth of different leaf shapes, sizes and colours, and many of them also have a long flowering season. A huge range of flower colours is available, giving you ample choice to suit any planting scheme.

Many perennials die right down in late autumn, re-emerging in spring, so they are useful for adding interest and colour mainly from late spring through to autumn. However, flowering times vary considerably, some blooming very early in the spring, others in late spring or summer, and some producing their display for late summer and autumn. Choose perennials for their coloured or interesting foliage and/or their flowers, taking care that they require similar conditions to any other plants you are mixing them with. You will find perennials suitable for all situations, including hot, dry sunny spots or shady corners, well-drained or moisture-retentive compost.

Perennials can be successfully combined in a large container to provide a display for much of the year. Massed displays of pots containing individual perennials are also attractive, as you can mix and match, swapping pots as some plants go out of season. When you are dividing and renewing perennials in your garden, pot some pieces up to give you a supply of plants throughout the year. They are excellent for popping in odd gaps in borders – in places where bulbs have finished, for example – to give you a further flowering display. Long-flowering plants such as hardy geraniums, penstemons, rudbeckias and campanulas are especially valuable for these situations, and they will intermingle well with surrounding plants.

By way of example, the following plants would provide a long-lasting perennial display suitable for a large pot of moisture-retentive compost in a shady or partially shaded spot. They would give you a wide variety of foliage types, from the bold fingered leaves of

hellebore to the delicate foliage of *Dicentra*, the rough-textured *Brunnera* and the grassy, almost black leaves of *Ophiopogon*. This selection would provide flowers from late winter through to mid-summer, and some of the foliage is more or less evergreen as well.

- ~ *Helleborus orientalis:* purple or pink, late winter–early spring
- ~ *Primula:* double white or deep blue, early–mid-spring
- ~ *Brunnera macrophylla:* sky-blue, early–mid-spring
- ~ *Ajuga reptans* '**Braunherz**': bronzed leaves; deep blue flowers, mid–late spring
- ~ *Anemone sylvestris:* white, mid–late spring
- ~ *Dicentra spectabilis:* pink, late spring–early summer
- ~ *Heuchera* '**Pewter Moon**': ice-pink, late spring–mid-summer
- ~ *Lamium maculatum* '**White Nancy**': variegated leaves, white flowers, mid-spring–early summer
- ~ *Ophiopogon planiscapus* '**Nigrescens**': almost black leaves, shiny purple berries, late summer–early autumn

Here are two examples for a sunny position, with completely different colour schemes. First, a long-flowering pink and white scheme with some silver foliage and a variety of flowers including both spikes and daisies:

- ~ *Geranium:* white or pink, late spring–autumn
- ~ *Veronica spicata* '**Heidekind**': deep pink, late spring–mid-summer
- ~ *Erigeron* '**Charity**': pink, early–late summer
- ~ *Aster* (**dwarf**): white or pink, late summer–mid-autumn
- ~ *Anthemis punctata* **subsp.** *cupaniana:* white, late spring–early autumn
- ~ *Iberis sempervirens* '**Schneeflocke**': white, mid-spring–early summer

OPPOSITE: *A colourful, exuberant planting of perennials in a large earthenware pot makes a vivid display in this corner, with a long-flowering* Geranium, *silvery* Festuca *and* Artemisia, *and fleshy, red-tinted* Sedum *to flower later in the summer*

Hardy geraniums are excellent additions to perennial containers, flowering over many months

Secondly, a yellow, orange and purple scheme, with contrasting foliage – tall, sword-like leaves, fine feathery leaves, textured leaves; flowers include spikes of *Salvia*, little round violas, long stems of *Crocosmia*:

- *Crocosmia:* orange, mid-summer–early autumn
- *Coreopsis verticillata* 'Moonbeam': soft yellow, mid–late summer
- *Euphorbia griffithii* 'Fireglow': flame-red, mid-spring–early summer
- *Salvia nemorosa* 'Ostfriesland': purple, early–late summer
- *Viola* 'Molly Sanderson': deep purple, spring–autumn

Perennials also mix particularly well with shrubs, grasses and bulbs to create a long-lasting, permanent display. The shrubs, whether they are evergreen or deciduous, will give a permanent framework as well as adding height, and may also provide flowers or autumn colour. Grasses will add extra texture and lightness to the planting, and spring bulbs create cheerful colour in the early part of the season. Summer-flowering bulbs are also useful in perennial arrangements, associating well among the varying foliage types. For example, *Allium* species are available in many sizes, including miniature ones for tiny plantings and others up to 20–30cm (8–12in) in height. Tall varieties with spectacular globular heads can be used for dramatic effect. Some have dainty, nodding heads of flowers, while others form dense, round globes. All add valuable summer and late-summer colour.

Grasses are particularly useful in plantings which contain a lot of solid foliage, as they create a more delicate texture by way of contrast. Depending on the variety chosen, a grass may also add height. Their later flowering is also advantageous, and the bleached heads of flowers as they are dying off can add to the display. Sedges are useful in collections in more moisture-retentive compost, and many are tolerant of shade so they mix well with plants such as *Brunnera, Lamium, Ajuga, Primula* and woodland *Anemone*. The foliage colours of sedges also add considerably to the effect.

Interesting foliage plants can be combined to create a display on their own, either in one container or in a group. Silver foliage plants are excellent together – as long as you vary the texture, shape and size of leaf so that they don't all merge into one big silver mass.

Artemisia, Achillea 'Huteri', *Dianthus* 'Dewdrop', *Tanacetum densum* subsp. *amani* and *Sedum spathulifolium* 'Cape Blanco' are lovely small plants with a variety of foliage which would mix well in a pan or small pot. This selection includes feathery, divided, fleshy, very fine and silky, and long, thin leaves.

For a larger display, the following would give you a mixture of cut, felted and silky leaves:

~ *Artemisia ludoviciana* 'Silver Queen' or
  A. absinthium 'Lambrook Silver'
~ *Stachys byzantina*
~ *Veronica spicata* subsp. *incana*
~ *Anthemis punctata* subsp. *cupaniana*
~ *Centaurea bella*

Contrasting foliage is important in perennial displays. Look at size, shape, texture and surface as well as colour. Consider the height of the foliage and the density of leaf cover. The possibilities range from plants with large, bold leaves down to those with tiny little leaves, and leaf shapes include rounded, pointed, feathery, divided, very fine, linear, oval, wavy-edged and spiky. Texture varies enormously: there are soft, felted leaves, sharp-edged, ribbed or deeply veined ones, and some which appear almost corrugated. Others can be puckered or wrinkled. Surfaces can be matt, shiny, woolly or smooth. Colours range from all shades of green to blue and blue-grey, silver, yellow and gold, bronze, purple and deep red. Some foliage is tinted or flushed, usually with reddish or purple hues over green. Variegated leaves should not be overlooked, but use them in moderation when combining with other plants.

You therefore have a wide range of options when using contrasting foliage. Mix bold leaves with spiky leaves, for example *Hosta* and *Iris*. Combine soft, rounded, felted leaves with finely divided and spiky leaves, such as *Alchemilla mollis*, *Coreopsis verticillata* 'Moonbeam' and *Sisyrinchium striatum*.

Think of the bold leaves of *Hosta* and *Bergenia*, the soft divided leaves of *Aquilegia*, *Dicentra*, *Thalictrum* and *Polemonium*, the smooth fleshy foliage of *Sedum spectabile* 'Brilliant' and *S.* 'Ruby Glow'. *Sisyrinchium*, *Crocosmia* and *Iris* provide linear, sword-like leaves, and *Heuchera* has wavy-edged leaves.

Perennials are excellent basket plants, and you can create a display for long-lasting effect in a hanging basket. You can use several plants of one variety to create a mass display, or a mixture of different perennials to give a longer season. You can also combine them with bulbs and small grasses. These, if well chosen, can give you almost year-round effect and colour; and again you can add bulbs, primroses or pansies for winter and early spring.

A basket of *Anthemis punctata* subsp. *cupaniana* looks stunning, with its silvery-green, finely divided leaves spilling over the rim. It is smothered in masses of daisy-like white flowers during late spring and early summer. If you then cut it back it will often flower again, though less profusely, later in the summer or in early autumn. *Alchemilla mollis*, or lady's mantle, is another good plant to grow on its own in a basket, with masses of soft, velvety foliage which looks good for much of the year, and sprays of tiny, greenish-yellow starry flowers over the summer months. Both of these plants will form a sizeable mass of foliage, hanging over the sides of the basket as well as forming a rounded dome above. Their flowers are borne all over the plant, so they will be noticeable from all around. Use three to five plants to each hanging basket, depending on the size of the basket.

An attractive perennial hanging basket can be made up using the following small plants:

~ *Sedum spurium* 'Variegatum': variegated pink and white fleshy leaves, pink starry flowers
~ *Geranium sanguineum* var. *striatum*: masses of pink flowers over a very long period
~ *Anthemis punctata* subsp. *cupaniana*: silvery leaves and white daisies
~ *Thymus herba-barona*: caraway thyme, with trailing, scented leaves and mauve flowers
~ *Nepeta* x *faassenii*: catmint, with soft mauve flowers

You could add a silvery-blue small grass, with pink or white dwarf tulips and white narcissi for their spring flowers. The rest of the basket would be in flower all through summer and early autumn, and the variety of foliage would keep it attractive for most of the year.

If you want to plant a perennial display in a window box, you will need to use small varieties, as most boxes are restricted in size and will not support large, strong-growing types. Large or tall plants would look totally out of scale anyway, as well as drying out too quickly and requiring a lot of feeding. Many perennial plants are available in small varieties, which can be used in smaller pots as well as in window boxes. Use the smaller, shorter grasses as well, to keep them in proportion.

Alpines

All sorts of alpines can be planted up in containers. Many are very tiny or require sharp drainage, and these can be provided for much more easily in pots than in the open ground. Pots also make them more visible, particularly if you only have a few; they can be placed where you can really appreciate them.

Small, compact types are best in pans, small pots, or sinks and troughs carefully chosen to suit their size. They can be grown either individually or as a collection or small landscape, as discussed in the next chapter. If they have specific soil requirements, these can easily be accommodated.

More robust alpines include those which are usually grown outside in rock gardens or raised beds, or even in the front of a border. These are suitable for planting in containers together with dwarf shrubs, small grasses or perennials, to which they will add contrast in shape, foliage colour and flower. They are perfect for carpeting beneath a deciduous shrub or filling in around the rim of a pot. You can also grow one or more types as a collection on their own. Use bushy thymes with coloured or lemon-scented foliage, long-flowering *Parahebe*, colourful *Helianthemum*, small *Dianthus*, aromatic *Achillea*, alpine *Campanula* and *Aquilegia*. These all associate well with dwarf shrubs and conifers and make the planting more interesting.

The trailing **Phlox subulata** *'Amazing Grace' tumbles over the side of a wooden planter*

This neat, compact **Phlox kelseyi** *'Rosette' is beginning to cover the edges of a sink*

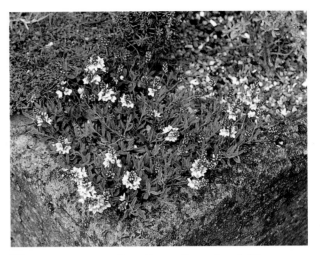

Veronica prostrata *'Rosea' is one of a number of alpine veronicas suitable for sinks or pans*

Trailing alpines are particularly attractive in mixed plantings to hang over the sides of pots, adding sheets of colour during their flowering season. Trailing *Gypsophila repens*, with its tiny white or pink flowers, is lovely with patio roses. Blue trailing *Veronica* is excellent with silver-leafed shrubs or perennials such as grey forms of dwarf *Hebe*, *Convolvulus cneorum* or *Dianthus*. Alpine veronicas are also lovely in a low pan on their own, forming a carpet as well as trailing over the sides, with pretty flower spikes in early summer. You will find pale and deep blue, white and pink varieties to ring the changes. Deep blue veronicas also look stunning with golden-leafed plants, or with gold and green variegated evergreens. For a different look altogether, plant them with deep purple foliage or flowers, perhaps adding a little white to lighten the effect.

Fleshy sedums are valuable in containers; many flower in the latter part of summer and into early autumn. Most have yellow, pink or white flowers, with foliage of green or purple, or sometimes variegated. They produce heads of starry flowers, relatively large, beloved by bees and butterflies. All of them are definite sun-lovers.

Bulbs

Bulbs are invaluable for adding seasonal colour and interest, particularly in early spring when there is little else in flower. They can be used in mixed plantings; either incorporate them when the pot is being planted up or, if it is the wrong time of year, push them in later. Take care to plant them deep enough. They are excellent with deciduous or evergreen shrubs, conifers or perennials. Provided you choose bulbs suited to the scale of the planting, there are endless possibilities.

Put miniature narcissi and irises in sinks, to keep in scale with other tiny plants. Dwarf tulips, narcissi, crocuses and scillas can be used in small pots; taller bulbs are better in large pots, with more substantial plants that will help to support their stems. You can either remove the bulbs when they have died down and plant them elsewhere in the garden, or leave them in the pot for the following season. Make sure in this case that you feed them well as they finish flowering and begin to die down, to allow the bulbs to build up reserves for next year's flowering. Don't tie up the leaves or cut them off, but let them die off naturally. Other plants in the pot can help to hide them, particularly if the foliage of perennials is beginning to grow through.

Tulips are not always successful for a second or third year; they tend to diminish, so are best replaced annually. Narcissi tend to keep going much longer.

A stunning display can be made in a single container with a mixture of bulbs, chosen so that their flowering times follow on from each other. Plant in layers so they are dense enough to make a really good potful. Use narcissi, tulips, hyacinths, crocuses and

These crocuses planted around a patio rose provide a splash of colour in spring

scillas or puschkinias. You can choose varieties of narcissi and tulips that flower at different times: in this way it is possible to have a pot of narcissi that will flower for several weeks, from late winter to mid-spring, or to have tulips in flower all through the spring months. A large container with a mixture of many bulbs can provide you with a spectacular display for weeks on end.

You can also create effective displays with groups of potted bulbs, using a single variety in each pot. Use different sizes of pot or bowl, with bulbs graduated in height. Crocuses, muscari and dwarf narcissi are excellent in low bowls or troughs. Dwarf tulips look wonderful massed in rounded pots or longer troughs. Taller bulbs are best in containers suited to their eventual height, and need sufficient depth to plant them in. You can use a limited colour scheme, such as cream and gold, or add blue for more impact. Alternatively you can have a blaze of colour with yellow, red, blue and white, or you can go for pastel colours of cream, pink and pale blue.

If you plant up lots of containers with individual varieties, you can bring them out when the bulbs start emerging and remove them when they have finished, thereby keeping your display fresh and colourful. Pots

of bulbs are also effective when grouped with pots of other plants, contributing colour and interest when the others may be looking a bit dowdy. They can add variety of shape and colour to a group, and again can be removed once their season is over.

Other bulbs worth considering include the forms of *Anemone coronaria* (strictly tubers, but sold as bulbs), with their wonderful silky, bowl-shaped flowers in velvety colours. Deep purple, scarlet or pink petals surround the large black boss of stamens in the centre, and the strong stems rise well above the ferny leaves.

Bulbs aren't restricted to spring, of course. Summer-flowering bulbs are very effective in pots on their own and are useful to place in spots where other plants have finished. They can be used to fill gaps in borders or to add to groups of other containers, or can stand individually in a prominent spot. Dwarf lilies look lovely for summer, with several bulbs to a pot, and are available in a range of wonderful colours. They are ideal for placing on the patio or near seating, or outside a door, where they can easily be admired and enjoyed.

Alliums are also useful, ranging from tiny alpine species up to tall spherical or conical-headed varieties. Individual bulbs can also be pushed into planted containers to liven up a planting in summer, bearing in mind that the majority of them require well-drained conditions and a sunny spot.

Individual pots of bulbs are a major element in this display, which uses carefully harmonized containers and flower colours

Bright mauve **Iris reticulata** *instantly cheers up this collection of shrubs and perennials in pots, and can be removed when flowering is over*

If you miss out on planting dry bulbs at the right time of year, don't despair: many are now grown in pots and sold by nurseries and garden centres as growing plants. You can transfer these carefully to your own container and still have a good display. Newly emerging bulbs can be separated and added to existing plantings, but as they get taller there is more risk of breaking the stems. Once the bulbs are growing it is best to plant them in their own pot, and either place them with other pots or keep them on their own, depending on the effect you want.

Think of the different flower colours and shapes. Tulips are available as elegant cup shapes, with pointed or fringed petals, or as double flowers. Parrot tulips have wavy-crested petals, and lily-flowered forms have reflexed, pointed petals. There are a huge number of different colours to choose from. Narcissi can have short or long trumpets and single or double flowers, and are available in all shades of yellow and gold with white and orange. The stocky flowers of hyacinths contrast with waving, elegant narcissi and the smaller tulips with broad, striped leaves, or the smaller heads of blue muscari.

Spring bulbs are also suitable for window boxes and hanging baskets, if you keep to the shorter kinds. Mix them with trailing ivy, primulas and pansies for a splash of spring cheer, or add a few to an existing planting of small varieties.

Herbs

Many herbs are hardy and perennial, and both culinary and ornamental herbs make colourful or fragrant additions to containers. Lemon-scented thymes, variegated sages and golden marjoram are all popular herbs that associate well with other sun-loving plants in well-drained containers. The purple and 'Tricolor' forms of sage (*Salvia officinalis*) are excellent with mauve, pink and white plants, while the gold and green 'Icterina' form goes with golden and deep green foliage

and yellow flowers, or alternatively with mauve. There are thymes with golden leaves, green splashed with gold, or green and silver, many of them lemon-scented. There is a marjoram with gold-splashed green leaves as well as a totally golden form. Herbs can be added to mixed plantings, or potted up individually to add to groups or to stand alone. The lower-growing forms of herbs look good in wide, low bowls or pans, with taller plants behind. They all associate well with sun-lovers such as lavender, *Cistus, Anthemis, Artemisia* and *Nepeta*. Put them on patios, near seats or outside doors, where you can catch their fragrance as you pass by.

Grow a collection of ornamental herbs in a pot, hanging basket or window box. Use *Salvia officinalis* 'Icterina', *Thymus* x *citriodorus* 'Golden Queen', *Origanum vulgare* 'Aureum' and *Melissa officinalis* 'Aurea' (variegated lemon balm). Add *Nepeta* x *faassenii* for its soft, harmonious colour, which looks lovely with the golden and green leaves and light mauve flowers of this scented display.

A pot of frequently used herbs is useful near the house, particularly by the kitchen door or at least within easy reach. You can plant up a large herb or strawberry pot or a long trough with rosemary, sage, chives and French tarragon. Put parsley (a biennial) in a separate pot next to it, as this requires a lot more water, and another pot containing lemon balm. Add any of your favourite herbs, and you have a whole herb garden to hand. You can add a pot of white- or purple-flowered lavender for more scent and colour, plus basil (an annual) later in the season, using varieties with frilled or purple leaves if you like.

Combine contrasting foliage shapes and sizes, for example the tiny rounded leaves of thymes, textured matt leaves of sages, hard, narrow leaves of rosemary and soft, linear leaves of chives.

OPPOSITE: *This containerized herb garden outside a back porch provides an easily accessible supply of culinary herbs for the kitchen as well as an ornamental display. An old tin tub has been put to use, with holes drilled in the base, and parsley and mint are also to hand in separate terracotta pots*

5

Planning your planting scheme

There are endless possibilities for designing planting schemes for every type of container. We will be considering sinks and troughs first, as their distinctive shape and relatively large size make them very versatile, and suitable for a wide variety of planting schemes.

Schemes for sinks and troughs

Sinks provide the ideal opportunity for creating a miniature landscape or displaying a special collection of plants. We will be looking at both possibilities, with several suggestions and variations.

Dwarf willows make excellent structural additions to sink plantings. Here, the clinging stems of Salix serpyllifolia *creep down the side of a sink*

MINIATURE LANDSCAPES
Mixed alpine landscape

A general miniature landscape can be made by combining one or two miniature conifers with a couple of dwarf shrubs and a selection of bushy, cushion-forming and mat-forming alpines. This gives you a pleasing mixture of heights, textures and colours, to which you can add evergreen and deciduous miniature trees and shrubs for more interest and variety. Smaller bushy plants provide shape, leaf and flower interest; cushion plants are useful for their neat, compact habit and for their flowers. Slow-growing carpeting alpines can be used to form ground cover, or they can trail over the sides of the container. You can also include tiny bulbs to grow through the carpeters – but do make sure they are in scale.

This type of planting gives interest and variety all year. The evergreens provide structure and colour even during the winter. Deciduous shrubs may show autumn leaf colour before the leaves fall, they may have interesting twigs or a good shape in winter, and you can watch the new growth unfurling in spring. Some, such as *Berberis* and *Spiraea*, have flowers as well, which gives them a long season of interest. Evergreen shrubs may have flowers and/or berries; examples include *Hebe*, *Cotoneaster* and *Berberis*.

Dwarf willows (*Salix*) include interesting gnarled upright forms, resembling weather-beaten trees, and creeping prostrate forms that may follow the contours of rocks or the sides of the sink. Many have the added attraction of fluffy catkins in spring. Shrubby alpines are also ideal for adding structure; these are tiny shrubs that remain woody above ground in winter but are on a very small scale, for example *Alyssum spinosum* and *Helianthemum lunulatum*.

Flowering alpines of all sorts can be chosen for their different flowering times as well as their variety of shape. Bushy alpines, with their upright or rounded shapes, add bulk and can contribute a great deal to the overall effect and interest of the planting, filling out the scheme and giving extra height. Many are more or less evergreen, and some have coloured foliage as well as flowers. They include some of the thymes and dwarf penstemons.

Tufted plants form neat clumps of foliage which originate from a central point; they often have long flowering periods. They contribute plenty of colour to the planting, often over a long season. Examples include dwarf asters, *Dianthus*, *Erodium* and *Sisyrinchium*.

Cushion plants form close domes of foliage tightly knitted together, often with minute flowers sitting right on top of the foliage. These include many desirable little alpines that are nonetheless totally hardy outside, for example *Silene acaulis*, *Minuartia*, *Scleranthus*, some *Dianthus*, *Asperula* and *Thymus serpyllum* 'Elfin'.

Rosette plants are those consisting of many rosettes of leaves packed closely together, forming mounds or

This mixed alpine planting includes a cheerful yellow Helianthemum lunulatum

Tufted and cushion alpines often provide colourful flowers and a long flowering season. This well-planted sink includes the cream-flowered Dianthus *'Nyewoods Cream'*

close carpets. They include the saxifrages, as well as the sempervivums and the closely related genus *Jovibarba*.

Mat-forming and trailing plants have prostrate stems that creep along the ground or hang over the sides; examples are veronicas, thymes, phloxes, *Hypericum reptans, Frankenia thymifolia* and *Gypsophila repens*. These are excellent for filling in around the taller plants and for softening the edges of sinks or rocks.

When using these plants to add varying dimensions to your scheme, take care to balance the overall effect. Arrange the plants in an interesting way, with mat-formers between taller plants; a rounded, bushy plant in front of a taller, spiky one; or plants with contrasting foliage next to one another. Before actually planting them, lay out the plants in their pots on the surface of the sink until you are satisfied with the result. Don't put the tallest one right in a corner or bang in the middle, but place it off-centre to look more natural.

Using rock or tufa to add substance, background and height can help to create the feeling of a real mountain scene. You can use just a couple of pieces to add interest, or arrange several pieces together and build up the soil between them to give more height and thereby extend the planting area. Don't just dot pieces of tufa over the surface – place them carefully so that they resemble a natural outcrop. This is easier to achieve with one or more largish pieces and a few smaller ones around the base, rather than using lots of little pieces. You can plant in all the crevices left between the tufa pieces, as well as in the gaps between the tufa and the edges of the sink, so don't worry about losing valuable planting space. Different kinds of chippings or grit can create various effects depending on their colour or size. Limestone chippings combine perfectly with greyish-white rock and tufa, as the colour is very similar. Granite or flint grit, in various brown and beige tones, blends well with sandstone rock. Slate can also be used, with slate chippings as a topping. The most important point is that you yourself are pleased with the result.

A newly planted sink freshly covered with hypertufa, showing tufa pieces and limestone chippings added as a topping

Realistic miniature landscapes and gardens

If you enjoy sink gardening, you may want to go one step further and create miniature landscapes or gardens that really do mimic their larger counterparts. This involves a lot more work and can be quite fiddly to construct, depending on how much detail you want to put in. However, it is a fascinating art, so long as the overall effect is kept in mind and you don't get carried away with too many extraneous bits and pieces. For all of these schemes, use the tiniest, slowest-growing plants you can, and don't include anything which might be at all invasive.

Rock garden

A few pieces of rock, with the strata running in the same direction, can be positioned to look natural. Place each rock one-third to two-thirds below the soil surface and firm the compost around them. Plant roots will revel in the moist, cool conditions beneath these. Plants are placed in the crevices between the rocks, keeping to very tight, compact forms. For the trees, use prostrate conifers and creeping willow to give a windswept effect.

Woodland scene

Use different varieties of trees – very miniature conifers are ideal – in groups of approximately the same height. Keep the design simple, adding a few woodland or carpeting plants such as primulas, violas, cyclamen, *Arenaria, Mentha* and dwarf narcissi. Use *Scleranthus* to mimic a mossy bank, and add one or two tiny dwarf ferns if you can find them.

Formal garden

Create paths from small pieces of flat stone, or use concrete and mark it while still soft to resemble a flagged pathway. You could make a symmetrical pool, and include clipped hedges and minute trellis fences. Trees should be tiny and symmetrical, and you could train miniature roses over an arch. If you use ornaments, do so sparingly and keep them tasteful: a sundial, birdbath, obelisk or statue are possibilities.

Informal garden

Here you can use *Scleranthus* to form grassy areas, tiny violas, primulas and other little alpines that remain compact, and a rustic trellis or fence. Use small *Sisyrinchium* to resemble irises, and tiny *Dianthus*.

Miniature knot gardens and topiary

You can extend the miniature garden theme by making a replica knot garden in a sink, using *Santolina chamaecyparissus* 'Small-Ness' or *Thymus* 'Peter Davis' as tiny hedging. These respond well to being clipped, so you can keep them neat and formal. Upright miniature conifers can be used for corner emphasis, as can clipped *Santolina* in ball shapes, or you can create more intricate miniature topiary shapes if you wish. Fill the areas between hedges with coloured gravel or tiny flowering alpines such as compact *Dianthus, Silene acaulis, Arenaria purpurascens* and *Asperula*.

Winter protection

The vast majority of the plants mentioned here are hardy and perfectly capable of being left out over winter. Some may look miserable in the cold and damp, but will soon shoot out again in spring. For those alpines that require winter or rain protection, the sink can easily be covered in some way, which is ideal if you do not have an alpine house or cold frame.

Late frosts may cause damage, or plants may die in a severe winter without the protective snow cover found in their native habitat. Use a piece of frost protection fleece on vulnerable plants in severe weather.

Rain protection is advisable only for plants that intensely dislike getting wet for prolonged periods (particularly over winter, when they are liable to stay damp continuously). These are usually very tight cushion plants, and plants with very soft or woolly leaves; prolonged dampness can rot these very quickly. The safest method is a sheet of glass firmly supported over the sink, or over the particular plant. This keeps the rain off but allows plenty of air to circulate, as a close atmosphere will also cause rotting.

Alpine collections

Very tiny or choice alpines are ideal for growing in a sink, where you can give them close attention and cater for their needs more easily. Collections can either be mixed or confined to plants of one genus.

A small fern, Woodsia polystichoides, *is part of a collection of shade-loving alpines in this sink, which is filled with peaty compost and placed in dappled shade*

Mixed collections

A variety of little plants requiring similar conditions can be grown together in a sink. Here are a few ideas:

Shade-loving plants for a sink in a shady position

This could include small ferns, forms of *Primula* x *pubescens*, dwarf willows, some miniature conifers, aquilegias and tiny ivies. All of these will thrive in a shady or partially shaded spot, in a peaty compost, and will give you a wide variety of foliage. Primulas and aquilegias will give a good show of flowers in early spring, while the evergreens provide interest all year.

Lime-hating plants in ericaceous compost

A lovely display of very dwarf rhododendrons, cassiopes and other lime-hating plants can be made in a sink, where it is easy to give them the growing conditions they need.

Plants from a specific habitat

You might like to collect alpines originating from a particular country or region of the world. As long as they all like the same conditions in terms of soil and position, they would make a uniquely satisfying and personal collection.

Lime-loving plants

You can add extra limestone to a compost mix for a selection of plants that prefer to have a higher level of lime in the soil, such as the silver saxifrages.

Plants that require extra-sharp drainage

There are many alpines that need very sharply drained soil to grow well. These include many of the silver foliage forms, and tight cushion plants. A compost mix can be made up which includes a high proportion of sharp grit or chippings.

Collections of plants belonging to the same genus

It is always fascinating to grow a selection of plants from the same genus together, as the variety and form within a genus can be very wide-ranging. They may vary in size, habit, foliage form and colour, flower colour and flowering period. You may like to consider some of the following suggestions:

Saxifraga

The very early-flowering types are ideal, having different rosette forms and a huge range of flower colours. They are immensely cheering near the house in

This collection of early-flowering saxifrages, some planted directly in tufa pieces, is contained in a shallow terracotta pan topped with limestone grit

winter and early spring. The rosettes usually form tight, compact cushions of green or blue-grey, sometimes encrusted with silver. Some form very hard pads of minute rosettes; others have somewhat needle-like leaves. They all flower extremely early, often in mid-winter, usually by late winter and into early spring. There is a huge range of flower colour: primrose yellow, bright golden yellow, white, pale pink, bright pink, apricot. There are many old and new hybrids to try in this category, and they usually flower reliably for years. There are masses to choose from, so view them in flower and pick those you like, or choose from a specialist nursery catalogue.

Silver saxifrages have rosettes of various sizes that are encrusted with lime, giving them a grey or silver appearance. They usually flower in late spring, with white, cream or pale yellow flowers on upright or arching stems, sometimes coloured red. There are also pink forms. They are often completely covered in sprays of flowers that last for quite a long time. They grow naturally in rock crevices, so try growing them between pieces of rock or tufa in your sink so that the flower stems can cascade. This is especially effective with *Saxifraga* 'Esther', *S.* 'Tumbling Waters' and *S.* x *canis-dalmatica*, which have masses of flowers on each arching stem, giving a wonderful frothy appearance.

There are many saxifrages to choose from: this early-flowering one is part of a whole collection in this sink

Varying rosette sizes and spathulate leaf shapes add interest to such a collection. (Spathulate leaves are broad and rounded at the tip, tapering to the base.)

For a mixed saxifrage collection, you could include both types. The tight cushion forms with an early flower display and the lime-encrusted rosettes with summer sprays could also be complemented by *S. oppositifolia* creeping and trailing down the sides, and *S.* 'Winifred Bevington' with green rosettes and airy sprays of pink-spotted white flowers. All thrive in a partially shaded position and are therefore ideal for growing together.

Dianthus

Alpine pinks are ideal for a sunny spot, with their neat hummocks of green, silver or grey foliage, and their flowers are often scented. They can form very low, tight domes or looser, tufted shapes, depending on the variety. Some produce soft-leafed domes, such as *D.* 'Nyewoods Cream', some are very hard and prickly mounds (*D. erinaceus*, the hedgehog dianthus), while others range from very tiny to larger tufted plants with longer leaves.

There is a tremendous variety of flower colour and style. Flowers can be single, semi-double or more fully double, and are often wonderfully scented. There are white, cream, red and all shades of pink flowers, sometimes two-tone or flecked with a second colour. Flowers can be almost stemless, just nestling on the foliage, or on dainty or sturdy stems held well above the leaves. All varieties usually flower in early summer, occasionally earlier, and sometimes sporadically until late summer.

Primula

There are many small varieties and cultivars suitable for growing in sinks. They provide a tapestry of colour in spring, being available in both pastel and strong colours including cream, white, mauve and purple, and their foliage sometimes has a mealy-white bloom. They need regular division to maintain them in good health (about every two to three years), and will in turn reward you with a colourful display every spring. They need a site with good light but out of fierce sun during the summer, so position them with care. A sink in partial shade is ideal.

Miniature ferns

Ferns can form a lovely collection in a sink placed in dappled shade; use humus-rich compost topped with fine bark or peat. Choose varieties with varying leaf fronds and different shades of green, and include some that are evergreen to give year-round interest. The unfolding fronds of new growth in spring are enthralling to watch, and the various shapes and patterns of the fully open fronds extend the interest into the year. Look out for the spores on the undersides of the fronds as well, and watch for new seedlings under your plants.

Sempervivums or houseleeks

Houseleeks are very effective when planted as groups, and will thrive as a collection in a sink. Include those with different-coloured rosettes, and notice how even individual leaf shapes are varied. Select contrasting ones for more interest. Rosette colours include apple green, olive green, yellow-green, bluish-mauve, red, deep red, mahogany, and others tinged or flushed with mauve, deep red or brown. Some change colour during the year, taking on their best colouring in the full sun of summer and dulling somewhat in winter's low light. Others take on red or orange tints in autumn and winter, almost glowing.

Sempervivums can be planted randomly, to give a pleasing effect with contrasting colours and sizes. They can also be planted in patterns, though this entails more maintenance, as you will need to remove or replace rosettes from time to time in order to keep the pattern accurate. This could be fun to do, particularly for the tidy-minded! The pattern can be as simple or as elaborate as you wish: either straightforward lines or blocks, or a knot garden effect with different-coloured varieties used as borders and fillings. Another possibility is to plant a circular border of one variety in the centre of the sink, fill with a contrasting-coloured one, and then fill in the remaining surface with another.

Sempervivums can look stunning planted in layers, alternating with long pieces of slate standing on edge. Keep to one variety in each layer, to give the appearance of stripes. This is a real refinement of the pattern technique.

Sempervivum varieties are fascinating to collect — this selection in a small wooden half-barrel shows a variety of rosette sizes and colours, creating a lively pattern

These are just a few suggestions, and you will be able to dream up many more, depending on your likes and dislikes. You may well find that you change your collections over the years as your taste changes. That is what gardening is about – growing, experimenting and changing. Don't think you have to stick to what you designed ten or even five years ago. If you are fed up with a certain plant or arrangement, and it no longer gives you any enjoyment, then change it. If you want to keep adding to your collections – after all, plant collecting can become quite an obsession – just acquire or make some more sinks.

Planting schemes for other containers

CHOOSING THE PLANTS

When selecting plants to use in containers, think about their overall effect, choosing plants either to complement each other or to form a sharp contrast with their neighbours. The best approach will depend on your type of container, where you are going to place it and what else is around it. You can think of it as landscaping your container, like a section of border on a smaller scale.

If you are planning a group of plants, either in one container or several, start by selecting plants that complement each other. Pick those with varying growth habits and with different shapes, textures and colours. Use a combination of upright, bushy and trailing plants to fill out the container; a well-filled container looks much better than one that is only sparsely planted. Use groups of smaller plants if necessary to fill it up. Place the taller plants off-centre, never right in the middle (except in the case of a specimen plant on its own in a pot). Add some trailing plants around the edges and then fill in with smaller, bushy plants.

You can add bulbs when planting up the container if it is the right time of year (late summer or autumn for spring-flowering bulbs, or spring for summer-flowering bulbs). Alternatively you can add bulbs to a ready-planted container, making sure that you push them in deeply enough. They will then emerge to grow through the other plants.

Shape

Plants with an extreme contrast of shape look attractive together, as each sets off the others. Dramatic plants are best in bold but plain containers. Spiky-leafed plants such as irises, *Sisyrinchium* and *Phormium* make a very effective contrast with rounded foliage mounds such as *Anthemis* and hardy geraniums. Plant feathery foliage with bold leaves, for example *Dicentra* with *Hosta*. Don't place very similar foliage types together or they will cancel each other out.

Feathery grasses with drooping flower panicles look effective next to bold leaves, glossy or woolly foliage or textured leaves. Use the various coloured forms of grasses in different arrangements; they are very versatile.

Shrubs with bare, woody bases can be disguised by planting smaller bushy types around them, or by using some kind of underplanting such as a prostrate dwarf shrub, ground-cover perennial or dwarf hardy cyclamen.

Colour

For complementary plantings you can use a number of different colour schemes, either in tones of one colour or in harmonizing colours. Consider both the foliage and flowers of plants you are using. Yellow and gold is always a cheering scheme, instantly brightening a corner. Mixed with green, it gives a warm glow to terracotta pots. Use a gold and green variegated plant as your starting point and add bright yellow narcissi, sulphur-yellow primroses and golden thyme.

Silver- and grey-leafed plants look wonderful in pastel schemes with pink, mauve and white, or more dramatic with purple or deep pink. If you use several silver plants, it is best to intersperse them with plants of different colours, or to use silver plants with different leaf shapes and textures. Many have fine, feathery foliage, and their charm will be lost if you put several together. A silver and white scheme is charming, particularly in a sunny spot or near seating, where it will be really effective at dusk. *Artemisia*, *Anthemis* and *Achillea* are all good silver plants for containers, as is the dwarf shrub *Convolvulus cneorum*.

Purple and yellow give a startling contrast, as does deep purple or black with crimson. Be sparing with combinations like this, and make sure they have a suitable backdrop. Deep purple *Salvia* in pots would look stunning in late summer in the border under crimson, red or orange *Crocosmia*, while the almost black leaves of *Ophiopogon planiscapus* 'Nigrescens' contrast with gold and green striped grasses or variegated *Euonymus*. The blue foliage of grasses, some dwarf conifers and hostas can be used to great effect among either pastel colours or hotter colours, and looks stunning with deep purple or cool with white.

Seasonal effects

Don't forget to think about plants for different times of the year. Bulbs, primulas, hellebores and winter-

An arrangement of pots for seasonal effect, with heathers, Iris reticulata, *hellebore and primrose for spring colour, added to a permanent collection of evergreen conifers and* Hebe

flowering heathers are obvious choices for spring, but there are also wonderful foliage plants. Try variegated or glossy evergreens, silver *Santolina* and bold sedges with bronze or striped leaves. Early-flowering saxifrages are invaluable for pans or small pots. Autumn brings amazing changes in foliage colour, so keep an eye out for dwarf forms of *Cornus*, small acers and *Nandina*. Combine with some bold evergreens and berried plants, plus late-flowering perennials such as dwarf asters and goldenrod. *Houttuynia cordata* 'Chameleon' is an excellent pot subject with its red, green and cream variegated leaves, flushed red in autumn. It dies down in winter, but combines well in late summer and autumn with the red-flushed and purple-tinted foliage of other plants. Many grasses are excellent in late summer and autumn with their dainty, feathery or

drooping flower panicles, giving contrast in shape and texture to more solid forms. Bronze, golden or variegated sedges (*Carex*) give outstanding value all year, retaining their colour throughout the winter. A quick tidy-up in spring, removing old leaves and trimming the ends, is all that is necessary to smarten them up for a new season.

SPECIMEN PLANTS

You may like to use plants as specimens in individual containers. Here are several ideas, many of which we have tried ourselves.

Many plants can be grown as individual specimens in a container, and displayed either alone or in a group. You may have a very attractive pot that you want to use for just one special plant, or you may simply prefer to have your individual plants in pots on their own rather than collected together.

Any plant you are fond of – such as a special plant that you have been given – may be treated as a specimen plant. Shrubs are ideal, and in fact many thrive better in pots on their own, where they have less competition for nutrients and water. However, imposing perennials and grasses are also effective alone. Try and make sure the container and the plant complement one another, and that the scale of the plant suits the size of the pot. Larger specimen plants are ideal as focal points or to make a statement,

The spotted, glossy leaves of Aucuba japonica *are ideal for brightening up a dark corner, as well as disguising the oil tank behind*

particularly if they are dramatic in outline or colour, or flower profusely.

To gain the most value from a specimen, choose a plant with a long season of interest. Evergreen shrubs with attractive foliage are an obvious choice, especially those with glossy, coloured or interesting textured leaves, or with variegation or other markings. Shrubs with a long flowering season are also valuable as specimens. Some examples of suitable specimen shrubs are suggested here; see the Plant Listing on pages 106–27 for more detailed descriptions.

Dwarf shrubs ideal for small or low containers

Cistus x *dansereaui* 'Decumbens': perfect for a hot, sunny spot, this low evergreen has dark green foliage and eye-catching large white flowers with a central crimson blotch.

Convolvulus cneorum: silky silver foliage and white, pink-flushed, funnel-shaped flowers all summer. Enjoys a warm, sunny position.

Dwarf shrubs suitable for small to medium pots

Hebe: the dwarf types are excellent for containers: several varieties have a long flowering season, they are evergreen, and some have flushed or tinted young growths and deeper colour in winter. Examples include *H.* 'Autumn Glory', *H.* 'Primley Gem', *H.* 'Nicola's Blush'.

Euonymus: there are many evergreen variegated forms of this invaluable plant.

Medium-sized shrubs for larger pots

Choisya ternata: distinctive, glossy, aromatic leaves and heads of extremely fragrant white flowers. Buds appear in very early spring, gradually opening in mid–late spring, and often continuing to appear during the rest of the year. This likes some shelter, so it is ideal in a container, where it will remain attractive all year.

Osmanthus: there are various types with leaves of different sizes and shapes, all slow-growing, and with extremely fragrant white flowers in mid-spring or autumn. Some forms are quite small, others are medium-sized bushes, so there is quite a choice for different-sized pots.

Euonymus alatus 'Compactus' is one of many dwarf deciduous shrubs, and its fiery red autumn foliage makes it an excellent specimen plant

Escallonia: most of these grow into large shrubs, but there are a few dwarf forms such as 'Red Elf' which make excellent container plants, with glossy, dense foliage and masses of flowers in summer.

Aucuba japonica: there are several named forms, all with attractive bold, shiny leaves variously marked or speckled. These are excellent shrubs for large containers, forming specimens as wide as they are high, and tolerating shady or partially shady positions. They are ideal for brightening up a dark corner or using in front of a dull hedge or fence.

Many shrubs have colourful spring or autumn foliage colours, and would make excellent specimen plants for their particular season. Examples include small forms of *Acer*, which make twiggy bushes or small trees in containers, the new unfurling leaves often having pink or red tints and the foliage turning yellow, orange, red or crimson in autumn. By pruning long stems back to two or three pairs of buds in late spring, acers can be kept to a manageable size and good shape. Other suitable shrubs with good autumn colour include most deciduous *Berberis*, dwarf *Cornus*, *Nandina domestica*, dwarf *Prunus* and *Euonymus alatus* 'Compactus'. The latter is a dwarf form of the spindleberry, and has incredibly fiery red autumn foliage. *Ceratostigma plumbaginoides* is a low creeping shrub suitable for a low, wide pot, and produces its deep blue flowers as the leaves begin to turn red, giving a stunning colour combination.

Many grasses and sedges make excellent specimen plants in larger containers, particularly those with silvery, golden, striped or bronze leaves. Some are upright with very fine leaves, others are more architectural with stiff leaves held out at an angle, while some form gracefully arching mounds. Flower heads can be light and airy, held well above the leaves, or drooping gracefully; or they can be fuzzy-textured

Specimen grasses and sedges can be grown in containers, and this imposing bronze form of Carex comans *has been placed near a garden bench*

spikes, or small, dense spikes held among the foliage. Some flowers are green or brown, becoming parchment- or buff-coloured as they age; others may be violet or black. Grasses and sedges are particularly effective placed on steps or patios to soften their hard surfaces and edges, or in borders to give contrast to surrounding plants. Make sure that arching types are put in a pot tall enough to show them off, or stand the pot on something – a step, an upturned pot or a low wall – to give it more height.

Specimen plants are best kept in tiptop condition: deadhead them regularly, removing broken or dead branches, and tidy away browned or fallen leaves. Topdress with some fresh compost at least once a year in spring, and again in autumn if you have time and they need it. Pot on into larger containers as soon as

they have obviously outgrown their current pot, and feed with a long-term fertilizer, as plants will soon deplete the nutrients in the compost. Fuller details on maintenance are given in Chapter 6.

Two or three specimen plants in separate containers placed together can give a long display if they are chosen carefully to follow on and to complement each other. The following examples will give you some ideas:

⌐ The glossy, dark green, spiny leaves of *Berberis* x *frikartii* 'Amstelveen' are bluish-white underneath, and this shrub has a dense, arching habit and yellow flowers. The wonderful old-gold foliage of *Hebe ochracea* 'James Stirling', with its tiny scale-like leaves, is complementary to this, the dense, outward-arching branches forming a low vase shape. The arching, striped green and gold leaves of *Carex oshimensis* 'Evergold' look good all year and give a contrast in texture. These evergreen plants are chosen for their good structure and the linked golden colour of foliage or flowers. All would make excellent specimen plants standing alone, but together they look even better.

~ A group consisting of dwarf myrtle, rosemary and lavender, each in separate pots, provides a common theme of evergreen aromatic foliage, varying in shape and colour but all having small, neat leaves. This selection gives you a long flowering season, starting with the rosemary in spring, followed by lavender in mid-summer and myrtle in late summer and early autumn. The colours harmonize well: white, soft blue, and mauve or pink.

~ Here is a group of evergreen shrubs to give you contrast in foliage colour and texture, linked by white in the flowers or foliage. *Euonymus fortunei* 'Emerald Gaiety' is a white and green variegated shrub, bushy or trailing depending on how much you cut it back, and with orange fruits on older plants. Contrast this with the rounded, stiff outline of *Osmanthus delavayi*, its dense, small, leathery foliage smothered in mid-spring by sweetly scented white flowers. These are set off by the low, deep green, crinkly-edged leaves of *Cistus* x *dansereaui* 'Decumbens', which also bears beautiful large, white, red-centred flowers all summer. Again, these could all stand alone as specimen shrubs, but put them together and they immediately enhance one another. You could add a low pot of a white-flowered *Erica carnea* to give extra interest over the winter.

MIXED PLANTINGS

You can plant up containers with a selection of plants, including any of the following, mixed and matched as you wish:

~ **Evergreen or deciduous shrubs** (dwarf or small)
~ **Dwarf conifers**
~ **Grasses and sedges**
~ **Small perennials or herbs**
~ **Robust alpines**
~ **Bulbs**

You can also include heathers, but make sure that any lime-hating ones are used with ericaceous plantings only. Many winter-flowering heathers (*Erica carnea* varieties) are suitable for ordinary compost; *Calluna vulgaris* varieties, which are intolerant of lime, are summer-flowering but usually have more attractive-coloured foliage.

Plants which are going to be put together in one pot must have similar requirements in terms of compost, drainage and position. The container needs to be large enough for the number and size of plants you want to include, but don't plant too sparsely or the effect will be disappointing. With regular feeding and watering, you can plant closely to give a full display, especially if some plants are trailing over the edges or forming a carpet on the surface for others to grow through. Bulbs can also form an additional layer, as they will push up through other plants.

While the plants are still in their individual pots, arrange them on the surface of the compost in your chosen container – or lay them out on a table or other surface – and move them around until you are satisfied with the effect. Then remove the plants from their pots and plant carefully into the compost. Put any dry bulbs in first, at the recommended depth, then put in the largest plants, filling in with smaller plants and those around the edges. If you don't have bulbs to hand at the time but want to add them, you can always push them in at a later date.

You can have great fun with mixed plantings, planning different combinations. One pot can contain a variety of plants to give some display for most of the year, or you can opt for a mixture that shows its full glory all at once. You can have a quiet, reflective scheme in subdued colours and tones, or a bright, cheery-coloured arrangement of one shade or many. You could include one or two plants as all-year-round background, with others to show interest and/or colour at various times. You can add splashes of colour by pushing in some primulas or pansies around the rim. Contrasts of texture, form, shape and foliage can be arranged, or you could try a harmonizing scheme of soft pastel flowers, or a bright arrangement of golden flowers and foliage. Choose schemes that suit both your personality and your garden.

Some particularly successful combinations we have used include the following, which you can easily follow or adapt.

1 shrub, 1 grass, 1 perennial:
~ *Hebe pinguifolia* 'Pagei', *Festuca glauca* 'Elijah Blue', *Veronica prostrata*
~ *Hebe* 'Nicola's Blush', *Festuca amethystina, Aster novi-belgii* 'Little Pink Beauty'

3 shrubs, 5 trailing alpines/perennials round edge:
~ *Potentilla fruticosa* 'Manchu', *Cistus* 'Silver Pink', *Santolina* 'Lambrook Silver' – *Veronica pectinata, Gypsophila repens, Saponaria ocymoides, Aubrieta, Thymus*
~ *Berberis thunbergii* 'Dart's Red Lady', *Ceratostigma willmottianum, Fuchsia* 'Mrs Popple' (hardy) – *Ajuga reptans* 'Braunherz', *Veronica prostrata, Campanula poscharskyana* 'Stella', *Geranium sanguineum* 'Album', *Sedum* 'Ruby Glow'

1 grass, 2 perennials:
~ *Carex oshimensis* 'Evergold', *Hosta* 'Halcyon', *Heuchera micrantha* var. *diversifolia* 'Palace Purple'
~ *Pennisetum alopecuroides* 'Hameln', *Coreopsis verticillata, Veronica gentianoides*

1 conifer, 7 alpines/bulbs round edge:
~ *Chamaecyparis thyoides* 'Rubicon' – *Anemone blanda, Muscari botryoides* 'Album', *Campanula carpatica* 'Blaue Clips', *Dianthus* 'La Bourboule', *Geranium dalmaticum, Veronica pectinata, Sedum* 'Ruby Glow'

1 shrub, 3 small perennials or alpines, 1 grass, 10 dwarf bulbs:
~ *Prunus incisa* 'Kojo-no-mai' – *Gypsophila repens, Veronica prostrata, Cyclamen hederifolium – Koeleria vallesiana* – 5 x *Galanthus nivalis*, 5 x *Crocus* 'Cream Beauty'

OPPOSITE: *A group of specimen dwarf shrubs and conifers, each individually potted, shows contrast in form, leaf shape and texture. A container of dwarf lilac has been added among them for colour*

~ *Euonymus fortunei* 'Canadale Gold' – *Alchemilla mollis, Nepeta* x *faassenii, Vinca minor* 'Alba Variegata' – *Stipa tenuissima* – 5 x *Narcissus* 'February Gold', 5 x *Crocus* (mauve)

How about making up a container for a special occasion as an unusual gift? Use a selection of plants with yellow and gold foliage or flowers for a golden wedding anniversary. Remember to include some dark green foliage to balance the gold colours. This would make a wonderful permanent reminder for the recipients. You could do the same for a ruby wedding, using dark red or purple-leafed plants, or some with red or crimson flowers, adding a little silver foliage to lighten the scheme. A silver-themed container is another possibility, using plants with silver foliage of various shapes and textures, or mixing some silver foliage and some plants with soft pastel or white flowers.

PLANTING FOR PARTICULAR POSITIONS
Containers can be planted appropriately for any situation in the garden. As before, make sure the plants you put together are happy in the same place. Here we give you some ideas and suggestions for particular locations in the garden.

Full sun
Use plants that flower really well in full sun, choosing compact varieties to give you blooms from spring right through to autumn; add bulbs and pansies for spring if you wish. Silver foliage plants are excellent; most of these revel in sunshine, and you can easily give them the extra drainage they require. Use sun-loving shrubs such as *Cistus* (sun rose), *Caryopteris, Cytisus* and *Genista* (brooms), *Lavandula, Santolina* (cotton lavenders) and *Senecio*. Dwarf hebes, patio roses, silver and blue grasses, and many perennials and alpines will add to your display. Pans of *Sempervivum* will be happiest in a really sunny spot, bringing out the richest colours in the rosettes.

~ *Convolvulus cneorum* is an excellent example of a small specimen shrub for a container in a sunny spot. It is a leafy evergreen with beautiful silky, silvery

A nicely weathered trough with a mixture of scented Dianthus *provides a summer display in this sunny spot*

foliage, enhanced during the summer months by clusters of white funnel-shaped flowers faintly flushed pink. It is a really lovely plant for most of the year, enjoying a warm, sunny position in well-drained compost. It would look stunning on its own in an attractive pot, but would also associate with contrasting deep purple foliage, or white and pastel-coloured flowering plants.

⁓ For a mauve, lilac and blue scheme, with contrast in shape and foliage, plant *Hebe* 'Primley Gem' and *Festuca glauca* 'Blaufuchs' with two trailing alpines, *Thymus serpyllum* 'Russetings' and *Veronica pectinata*.

⁓ A golden scheme could see *Euonymus fortunei* 'Golden Pillar' as a centrepiece, its dense green and gold foliage instantly cheering, surrounded by the small, bushy, golden-flowered *Hypericum olympicum*. Some dwarf yellow narcissi pushed in around these will enliven the planting in spring.

⁓ A group designed for colour contrast might include the autumn-flowering *Ceratostigma plumbaginoides*, with its stunning deep blue flowers enhanced by the red autumn tints of the foliage, with the airy, fine-leafed grass *Festuca amethystina*. The purple flower heads of the latter droop gracefully, and you could also add a deep rose-coloured rock rose, *Helianthemum* 'Ben Ledi'.

Shade

Use dwarf shrubs that tolerate shade, with trailing ivy, *Vinca* or *Ajuga*, together with early bulbs and hardy cyclamen for spring and autumn flowers. Snowdrops and species crocus (which tend to be daintier than modern hybrids) are ideal under deciduous shrubs, especially with a carpet of cyclamen leaves or low evergreen ground cover such as *Euonymus* or prostrate *Cotoneaster*. There are numerous perennials that thrive in shade, so exploit their potential and have a pot full of different ones that go well together, as in the third example below.

⁓ The dwarf dogwood *Cornus stolonifera* 'Kelseyi' has dense red and yellow twigs throughout winter, revealed as the red-tinted autumn foliage falls away. This is enhanced by trailing green ivy, the marbled foliage of *Cyclamen hederifolium* which also flowers in autumn, snowdrops pushing their way through in spring, and white primulas, which often have bronzed leaves to add to the effect.

⁓ *Viburnum opulus* 'Nanum' is a very dwarf guelder rose, with dense, twiggy red branches, forming a rounded shrub. It has attractive new spring growth and autumn colour, and looks effective underplanted with the prostrate *Euonymus fortunei* 'Minimus' and autumn-flowering *Cyclamen hederifolium*.

⁓ This collection of perennials in a container would give you a variety of foliage shapes and colours, together with lots of different flowers from early spring through until summer. *Helleborus* x *sternii* would form a focal point, with the large textured leaves and blue flowers of *Brunnera macrophylla* forming a good foil. *Ajuga reptans* 'Braunherz' has mats of deep purple leaves which trail as well, and spires of blue flowers, contrasting with the spotted foliage of *Pulmonaria* and silvery green leaves of *Lamium maculatum* 'White Nancy'. A lot of the interest in this planting would come from the variety of foliage, in addition to the flowers at different times.

⁓ A planting for spring interest in shade could include *Mahonia aquifolium*, with purple-tinged, glossy, leathery leaves and heads of bright yellow flowers, together with white *Helleborus niger*, a double primula and some dwarf narcissi. This gives you sharp foliage contrast and stunning flowers over a long period in spring.

Exposed positions

Here you need plants that are extremely hardy and will tolerate cold, wind and draughts. Low-growing plants are ideal, as they are less likely to topple over than taller ones. Plants with thick, leathery leaves are excellent. There are many evergreen shrubs that will tolerate exposure, including *Euonymus*, *Berberis*, *Aucuba* and *Cotoneaster*. Some conifers are also suitable, particularly

An excellent combination for a shady planting, this stunning double primrose, Primula 'Miss Indigo', *planted under white* Helleborus niger, *provides a long display in spring*

junipers and mountain pines (*Juniperus* and *Pinus mugo*). Add some low-growing perennials such as geraniums, and small sedges (*Carex*), which are very tough.

The dwarf birch *Betula nana* makes an excellent specimen shrub, and is totally hardy. It forms a low, bushy shrub or a small tree, depending on how much you prune it, and has tiny leaves and catkins in spring.

The green and white foliage of *Euonymus fortunei* 'Emerald Gaiety' is tough enough to withstand exposed positions, and associates well with white or mauve geraniums which would give you colour for long periods.

A lovely coloured foliage combination would be a planting of the deciduous red-leafed *Berberis thunbergii* 'Dart's Red Lady' together with the small, glossy leaves of *Cotoneaster procumbens* and the blue needles of *Juniperus squamata* 'Blue Star'. The yellow flowers of *Berberis* and red berries of *Cotoneaster* add further interest.

Sheltered gardens

You can grow all sorts of plants in a sheltered spot, including those that are on the borderline of hardiness or are usually cut back in a hard winter; in a sheltered position they are likely to look better for longer. Plants with large, soft foliage are best in sheltered spots, as are those with silver or woolly leaves. Hardy fuchsias and *Phygelius* are best given some shelter, particularly in pots, as the roots are more vulnerable to frost than if they were deeply buried in the soil and mulched.

Patios

You will want your containers to be attractive, colourful and full – particularly for the times you spend relaxing or dining in your garden, which will probably be mostly during the summer. Have some flowering shrubs and plenty of perennials that flower throughout the summer, swapping some pots for others if they have finished or are beginning to look tired. If you have pergolas or posts, you can add to your display with hanging baskets. Fill a basket with trailing alpines, *Dianthus*, dwarf *Hebe* or *Euonymus*, *Geranium*, *Veronica* and *Sedum* to give you colour all through summer and autumn. Summer-flowering bulbs such as pot lilies can be used, and striking specimen plants such as *Phormium* are ideal in strategic spots. Dwarf irises are excellent in containers, and are lovely even though they have a short season. Use attractive grasses or sedges in containers, and later-flowering plants such as *Sedum*, *Geranium* and *Hebe recurva*, with smaller *Crocosmia* cultivars and dwarf asters to prolong the display.

Around seating areas

Seating areas are the ideal places to use scented plants, particularly if you like to sit out in the evenings, when scent is often stronger. Ornamental and culinary herbs are invaluable, as well as all forms of lavender, silver foliage plants, and plants with flowing stems and frothy masses of flowers. White flowers are excellent, as they show up well during dusk. Some recommended plants to use are *Lavandula angustifolia* 'Imperial Gem', a deep purple neat form, with *Salvia officinalis* 'Tricolor', a sage with striking purple, pink and white leaves. A good companion would be *Anthemis punctata* subsp. *cupaniana*, with spreading silver dissected foliage and a long succession of white daisy-like flowers.

Outside doors

This is a good place to impress visitors, as well as enjoying the sight yourself, so use groups of well-maintained plants or one or two well-chosen combinations of plants in attractive containers, adding seasonal plants if you wish, or swapping with fresh containers as necessary. Bulbs are brilliant for spring, and you can also use evergreen and flowering shrubs, dwarf conifers and small flowering plants. Scented plants are lovely in summer – place them where you can brush against them as you walk past.

SEASONAL ADDITIONS AND CHANGES

Permanent container plantings, however well planned, can end up looking duller than you would like at certain times of the year. You can liven them up by using seasonal plants or bulbs, which can be removed once they are finished.

If you plan your container in advance and plant up in the autumn, you can add dry bulbs at the time of planting, which can then be permanent and give you colour year after year. You can pull them out after flowering if you prefer – although this may be quite difficult as they will be low down in the pot. If you decide to add bulbs to a container at a later date, either

Primroses are invaluable for adding spring colour to pots. These pale yellow ones cheer up a variegated Euonymus

plant dry bulbs at the appropriate time, or add growing bulbs in early spring.

Many garden centres and nurseries now sell pots of bulbs ready growing, which are ideal to pop into ready-planted containers. You can separate the bulbs (they are usually sold three per pot), taking care not to damage the roots, and plant them around or among other plants in your container. Dwarf narcissi in yellow, orange and white, small crocuses in mauve, cream or yellow, *Iris reticulata* in blues and purples, and white or blue *Muscari* are all instantly cheering for spring. You can also use little blue or pink *Scilla*, and *Anemone blanda* with its long-lasting flowers in all shades of blue and mauve, plus pink and white. Dwarf tulips are excellent, particularly those with dashing red and orange colours. These additional bulbs can either be left in your container, or removed when finished and planted elsewhere in the garden. If you buy them when newly emerging or in bud, you can still have several weeks of enjoyment from them, so it is well worth the effort.

Primroses are also wonderful for spring colour. There are masses of colours to choose from, including bicolour forms and double varieties, so you can find ones to suit any planting scheme. They will flower for weeks and again can then be lifted out and planted elsewhere if you wish.

Bulbs can, of course, also be used for summer colour. In larger containers you can use lilies, alliums and camassias.

You can add cheerful winter-flowering pansies or small violas, again just choosing whatever colour will suit, and popping them in around other plants or round the rim of the pot. Small hardy cyclamen are excellent in permanent plantings, particularly when underplanting a shrub or included with other small woodland perennials. *Cyclamen hederifolium* has marbled or silvered leaves, and flowers in autumn. The pink or white snout-nosed flowers are followed by the leaves, which give wonderful foliage cover and interest. The little winter cyclamen, *Cyclamen coum*, produces dainty flowers of pink, maroon or white throughout the winter months, and has rounded leaves of silver or green, often attractively marked. Both of these species add interest round the base of a shrub, particularly a deciduous one, as they provide a display while the shrub is doing little. Add a few snowdrops as well for further early spring colour, and you will enjoy this sort of planting all year round.

Additions of bulbs, pansies, primroses and cyclamen are especially useful with deciduous shrubs or herbaceous plantings, which can otherwise be rather bare in winter and early spring.

If you want to liven up or add colour to a planting or a group of pots, but don't want to disturb the existing plantings, you can just as easily place separate pots of bulbs or primroses around, among or in front of your other containers. Use a whole potful of your chosen seasonal plant to give maximum impact, or plant one or more types together in a container.

Colour schemes

Container gardening offers great scope for choosing plant combinations with a particular colour scheme. It is easier to plan a colour scheme when you are working with a limited number of plants than when working on a large border. Even if you are only using two or three plants, picking certain colours or shades to go together can create a restful, harmonious look, a bright, vibrant show, or a startling contrast. You can also assemble planted containers together to make an attractive colour group. Flower, foliage and container colours can

be chosen to contrast or harmonize. When planning container schemes, we find it helpful to think about the following points.

SHAPE AND COLOUR OF FOLIAGE
The leaves of plants show a huge variety of sizes, shapes, textures and colours. Think of the velvety rounded leaves of lady's mantle (*Alchemilla mollis*), the swordlike bronze or purple leaves of *Phormium*, the glossy, leathery foliage of *Mahonia aquifolium*, the narrow, aromatic grey leaves of lavenders and the deeply textured foliage of primulas. Leaves may be entire, divided, feathery, narrow, broad, needle-like, rounded, pointed or grassy in shape. They can be leathery, thin, glossy, matt, woolly or smooth.

The shape and colour of foliage in autumn is illustrated by the bright crimson and yellow tints of this Japanese maple, a small-leafed form of Acer palmatum

Leaf colours include all shades of green, blue-green, yellow-green, gold, yellow, silver, grey, blue-grey, purple or dark red. They may be variegated or striped – usually green and white or green and gold, but some have pink or purple variegation, as in *Sedum spurium* 'Variegatum' and *Salvia officinalis* 'Tricolor'. Leaves do change colour through the year, so take advantage of this as well. New growth is often paler or pink-tinged, deepening in colour as it matures. Newly unfolding leaves are often bronzed, pinkish or red in colour, and may be pleated or folded before they unfurl. Some plants have darker or red-tinted young growths. Autumn colour is another exciting aspect. Many plants show autumn tints in their foliage – particularly deciduous plants, which often have dramatic, fiery autumn colours. Some evergreen plants also show deeper or different colours during colder weather.

Foliage can be exploited by using it on its own or as a background for flowering plants; or various foliage forms can be combined together. Don't think of foliage merely as a backdrop; it has a much more important role to play in the overall effect you want to achieve. Bold leaves are excellent for setting off more fussy-looking plants and creating a calming influence; they also combine well with smaller-leafed foliage plants for contrast. A container can be made up of a mixture of attractive foliage forms alone.

Background foliage should be chosen to give structure and form to the planting as a whole. You can use strong upright forms such as *Iris, Phormium* and *Crocosmia*; the bold, broad leaves of hostas; the textured, crinkly leaves of *Tellima* and *Primula*; and the soft, felted leaves of *Alchemilla*. In smaller-scale schemes for sinks and pans, *Sisyrinchium* and dwarf irises provide upright leaves, and you can contrast these with fleshy *Sedum*, the needle-like leaves of *Phlox* and the minute foliage of alpine thymes.

FLOWER COLOUR

For a mixed planting, choose flowering plants that complement and harmonize with each other. Bold, strong colours or large flowers are best used on their own, or as part of a strongly contrasting arrangement with equally bold foliage. You don't have to use a single colour, as each area of the spectrum has a wide range of shades that will tone beautifully. For example, a range of blues and mauves will mix well, or soft and deep pink, or hot reds and bronze, or cream, yellow and gold. Using a limited range of toning colours is an ideal way to create harmonious container plantings, particularly if you are not too sure of what will mix successfully.

EXTENDING THE FLOWERING SEASON

You can design a mixed container planting with plants that all flower together, or with flowering periods that spread over several months. If you are using several containers with single plants in each, you can easily move them around and replace them as new plants come into flower.

Single-season plantings can be extremely effective. A dwarf *Forsythia* with small yellow and orange narcissi looks cheerful in early spring, while green-flowered hellebores, yellow narcissi and mauve primulas or violas give a long-lasting spring display.

Hardy geraniums are excellent long-flowering plants for containers, whether used as part of a group, or planted around the sides of larger pots. Use blue and mauve forms with silvery artemisias, purple sage, white lilies or irises, to give harmonizing colour schemes with contrasting foliage shapes and textures. White geraniums and purple campanulas complement each other beautifully, and you can use larger perennial forms of each, or the smaller alpine forms for a little pot.

Deep pink Dianthus *and white* Minuartia *complement each other perfectly in this sink planting*

An effective container planting with a long spread of flowering season. The narcissi are prominent in spring, followed by blue spires of Ajuga, *then lilac spikes of* Hebe *in summer. The deep green and purple foliage of these plants provides a background all year round*

For flowering over a long period, use a dwarf *Hebe* such as *H.* 'Autumn Glory', which produces its deep purple spikes over late summer and autumn, together with a carpet of *Ajuga reptans* 'Braunherz' to provide purple leaf colour and bright blue spires in spring. The *Hebe* foliage turns deep purple over winter, giving an even stronger colour scheme. Add trailing *Veronica peduncularis* 'Georgia Blue', which has small bronzed leaves (green in summer) and rich blue, white-eyed flowers in mid-spring and sometimes also in autumn.

If you have one or two mixed container plantings, it is a good idea to try and spread the season of interest to give you as much of a display as possible over a period of time. This is equally feasible with a particular colour scheme, especially if you choose plants in toning shades. Alternatively, if you have several containers, you could have groups with plants all looking their best at the same time, or over a period of time, perhaps swapping some as new plants come into their own.

SOME IDEAS FOR COLOUR SCHEMES IN YOUR CONTAINERS

Silver foliage always harmonizes beautifully with pink, mauve or white flowers, creating a soft, gentle look. Silver filigree foliage is particularly pleasing in such schemes. A bolder look can be achieved by using pink and magenta flowers with silver foliage. A mixture of silver foliage plants with a variety of textures is another stylish possibility. Combine bold or entire leaves, feathery foliage and finely dissected leaves.

A golden dwarf Spanish gorse and brightly variegated lemon balm with a dark green Hebe, *all grown in individual pots, create a stunning colour group outside this greenhouse*

Silver or grey foliage can lift a planting by highlighting deeper colours planted with it. Create an impact by using it with deep purple or magenta. White flowers and silver foliage is always a pleasing combination, making the white appear purer by contrast. You could also try mixing silver foliage with dark red or purple-leafed plants, which will again be enhanced by the association.

Pastel colour schemes are easy on the eye and very attractive. Use foliage or flowers in toning shades of soft pink, lavender and white. Try purple sage with a white *Dianthus* and pink *Gypsophila* to trail down the side of the pot. Use *Geranium sanguineum* var. *striatum*, *Veronica spicata* 'Heidekind' and a dwarf pink aster, all in varying tones of pink, to flower all through the summer and autumn. A soft pink patio rose underplanted with white crocuses and carpeting thyme carrying soft mauve or pink flowers will give you a harmonious colour scheme with a good spread of flowering season.

Another soft, light scheme that is always restful consists of white or cream variegated foliage combined with plain green. The variegated leaves lighten the overall effect, whether you are using alpines, perennials or shrubs. Good choices include *Euonymus fortunei* 'Emerald Gaiety', *Iris pallida* 'Variegata', several ivies, hostas, *Lamium* and *Pulmonaria*, and some grasses and sedges. There are several different leaf shapes, sizes and textures within this selection as well.

Variegated plants are best used sparingly, with plain colours for contrast, as too many variegated plants together lose their individual attractiveness and can even appear sickly. Use white and green variegated foliage with dark green, fresh or light green, and blue-grey leaves, and white, pastel or purple flowers. Deep red is another effective contrast. Gold and green variegation looks stunning with golden-yellow, orange or primrose-yellow flowers, and also with deep purple. It can brighten any dark green foliaged plant, and combines well with yellow or golden foliage as long as there is sufficient green to set the scheme off.

Yellow and golden foliage will brighten a planting scheme or a dark corner, but is best used in small amounts. It is stunning with dark green or dark purple foliage. Golden shrubs include *Hebe ochracea* 'James Stirling', *Physocarpus opulifolius* 'Dart's Gold' and *Spiraea japonica* 'Gold Mound'. *Lysimachia nummularia* 'Aurea' is an effective golden-leafed trailing plant, and there are several grasses and sedges with gold leaves. Purple foliage can be found on *Berberis thunbergii* 'Dart's Red Lady' and the perennials *Heuchera micrantha* var. *diversifolia* 'Palace Purple', *Ajuga reptans* 'Braunherz' and *Ophiopogon planiscapus* 'Nigrescens'. Many shrubs show deep purple or red coloration in young growths, or on leaves during winter, and many perennials have purple-tinged foliage. An exceptional combination in a single plant, which would make an eye-catching container plant, is *Ranunculus ficaria* 'Brazen Hussy', with its deep bronze-purple leaves topped with brilliant golden buttercup flowers which open fully in the sun.

A stunning, vivid colour combination would be dark purple and lime green flowers and/or foliage together with golden foliage. A dramatic colour scheme such as this is best used sparingly or in small groups for impact. Red, crimson, bronze and purple foliage looks stunning, but in large quantities can appear sombre. Mix bronze and purple foliage with crimson flowers, or hunt out foliage plants in these deeper hues.

OPPOSITE: *This soft and harmonious colour scheme combines mauve-flowering alpines with a blue-grey* Sedum

6

Preparation

It is very important to prepare your containers properly before planting anything; well-prepared containers will last and remain functional for many years. This chapter covers all kinds of preparatory work, from making or adapting the container itself to providing appropriate drainage and compost for your chosen plants.

Making and adapting containers

COATING A PORCELAIN SINK

While plants will grow quite happily in a glazed white sink, the colour makes the feature very stark and obtrusive. Coating the sink to achieve a more natural stone effect makes it easier to blend in, and helps it to weather and develop an aged look.

The best material for coating is a mixture of sand, peat and cement, frequently called *hypertufa*, as it is sometimes used as a substitute for the naturally occurring rock tufa. Coating your first sink will probably take an hour or two, so allow yourself plenty of time and pick a settled day, without bright sun or rain forecast, if possible.

The procedure is as follows:

1   Remove any old plumbing fittings still attached to the sink. If these are very old they may need to be carefully cut off using a sharp hacksaw.
2   Thoroughly wash and clean the sink with detergent, taking particular care to remove any oil or grease.
3   Allow the sink to dry, or wipe it dry.
4   Move the sink as near as possible to its final position before starting the coating process, as the hypertufa can be easily chipped by moving the sink.
5   Mix up some plasterer's bonding agent (PVA adhesive) according to the instructions; an average-sized sink will need about 2–3 tablespoons of bonding agent. When it is mixed, add a small handful of sand to the mixture and stir in well.
6   Stirring the mixture all the time, coat the outside of the sink and about 5cm (2in) down the inside. Allow the coating to dry thoroughly. The sink should now have a sandpaper-like texture all over. This rough surface makes it much easier for the hypertufa mix to adhere.
7   The hypertufa mix is prepared by mixing the following (by volume):
    ~ 1 part peat
    ~ 1 part sand
    ~ 1 part cement
    Add sufficient water to give a smooth, firm texture. Make sure you mix enough, as the colour of every batch varies slightly. If you want to make the mixture slightly harder, then decrease the amount of peat; this is a good idea if the sink is likely to be knocked or moved a lot. If there are lumps of peat in the mixture, don't worry about them, as these add extra texture. The final colour of the coating will depend on the type of sand used, and we have found that red pit sand gives a pleasant dark colour.
8   The coating process will take a little practice (unless you happen to be a plasterer by trade). The mix should be transferred to the sink using a builder's trowel, and it will adhere better if it is gently pressed onto the surface. Work from the top downwards, bringing some of the mixture over the inside lip to help to secure it in place. The mix should be taken down about 5cm (2in) inside the sink so that when it is filled with compost none of the porcelain is visible. Take the mix underneath the base of the sink a little as well. Leaving a rough surface will improve the appearance of the finished sink and help speed up the weathering process.
9   Once the coating is finished, the mixture needs to be left for about a week to harden thoroughly before filling and planting. If rain threatens during the first day, gently cover the sink with some polythene. A box placed in the middle helps to keep the polythene away from the edges of the sink.

Coat the outside of the sink with PVA adhesive mixed with a little sand

Transfer the hypertufa mix to the sink using a builder's trowel

The completed sink, showing how the hypertufa is taken a little way down the inside

10 A filled sink is very heavy, so it needs a firm base. If the site has been recently dug, the soil under the supports should be firmed as much as possible to prevent it sinking.

11 Sinks need to be placed on supports which are high enough at least to allow water to escape from the drainage hole. The exact height can be chosen to suit the situation. Standard building bricks are ideal, raising the sink about 7–10cm (3–4in) and blending reasonably well with the hypertufa covering. Concrete building blocks can also be used where more height is required. Place the supports a little way in from the edges of the sink so they are not too visible, and take care not to block the drainage hole.

MAKING HYPERTUFA CONTAINERS

Casting in hypertufa can produce an interesting variety of containers. The range of shapes you can make is limited only by the types of mould you have to hand or can get hold of.

To make a mould you need two similar-shaped containers, one of which is about 4cm ($1^{1}/_{2}$in) smaller than the other all round. Moulds can be made out of wood, but containers cast in these often need a lot of subsequent work to soften the very sharp angular corners produced.

One of the best methods is to use two cardboard boxes. These tend to sag and become uneven as they absorb moisture during the casting process. The resultant containers have unique shapes and curves, looking much more natural.

CASTING FROM CARDBOARD BOXES

1 To improve the strength of the finished container, the hypertufa mix needs to contain a higher proportion of sand than would be used for coating a porcelain sink. The ideal proportions are (by volume):
  - 2 parts sand
  - 1 part peat
  - 1 part cement

2 Choose two boxes such that the smaller one will allow a gap of at least 3cm ($1^{1}/_{4}$in) all round when placed inside the larger one.

3 Place the outer box on a firm surface and fill with a 4cm (1½in) layer of the hypertufa mix. Level and compact this with a builder's trowel. To make the drainage holes, press a 4cm-long section of broom handle (or similar) into the centre of the base. Longer troughs should have two or three holes made in this way.

4 If the container is more than 30cm (12in) long it is a good idea to reinforce the base by placing some wire netting in the cement mix. Half-fill the base with hypertufa, place the netting on top and then add the rest of the hypertufa mix.

5 Now place the smaller box in the middle of the base and hold it in place with a brick or similar weight. Add more hypertufa mix into the gap between the two boxes, firming it down so that it becomes continuous with the base and contains no air pockets. As you do this, the cardboard boxes will begin to sag. If the outward movement becomes too great, place some bricks or similar heavy objects around the box to provide some support. The hypertufa mix should be levelled off with the top of the lower box.

6 Once the casting is complete, leave the container to dry until the mix is firm to the touch but can be scratched with firm fingernail pressure. This usually takes one or two days, depending on the weather. If working outside, the sink can be covered with polythene if rain threatens – but place something round the sink to keep the polythene from touching it. A small trough could be made up on a board so it can be moved inside if necessary.

7 Once the hypertufa is dry, the cardboard can be gently torn from the container, and the pieces of wood used to make the drainage holes can be carefully removed from the base. A gentle brushing will remove any shiny surface and marks from the cardboard, leaving a rough surface that will speed up the weathering process.

8 The container should then be left for one or two weeks to harden fully before planting up. Small hypertufa troughs can be supported on thin pieces of brick or slate, or raised higher on half-bricks if you prefer, to ensure that the drainage hole is kept clear of the ground.

WEATHERING COATED SINKS AND HYPERTUFA CONTAINERS

Newly coated or cast hypertufa containers can look very hard and cold, and although they will naturally weather over a period of time, we have found that painting the surface with a dilute solution of yoghurt or liquid manure can speed up the process. This will encourage the growth of moss, lichen and algae, particularly if the surface is kept damp. This softened appearance is particularly effective on sinks that are in the shade at least some of the time.

WOODEN CONTAINERS

Wooden containers can be either formal or informal, depending on how they are made and used. Simple containers can easily be made by anyone with basic do-it-yourself skills.

The easiest types to make are simple designs using sawn timber. To help ensure a long life, use pressure-treated timbers sold for fencing. Two simple designs are shown in the diagrams opposite.

In order to prolong the life of a wooden container it needs to be treated thoroughly with a penetrating wood preservative, paying particular attention to the end grain. For the first treatment, a preservative that needs to be left to dry before planting is usually more effective. Once the container is established, an annual treatment with a good preservative that is harmless to plants will maintain the appearance and extend the life of the container. You can use a stiff brush beforehand to remove old compost, algae build-up and general dirt.

PREPARING AND ADAPTING OLD CONTAINERS

The choice of objects that can be used as plant containers is limited only by the imagination. The only requirements are that the container must hold compost, allow water to drain away, and not be toxic to plants. There are also aesthetic considerations – we don't believe old tyres (painted or otherwise), old toilet bowls or polystyrene containers can ever look other than they are!

With many items the biggest problem can be drainage, but even this can usually be overcome by careful drilling with the appropriate drill bit.

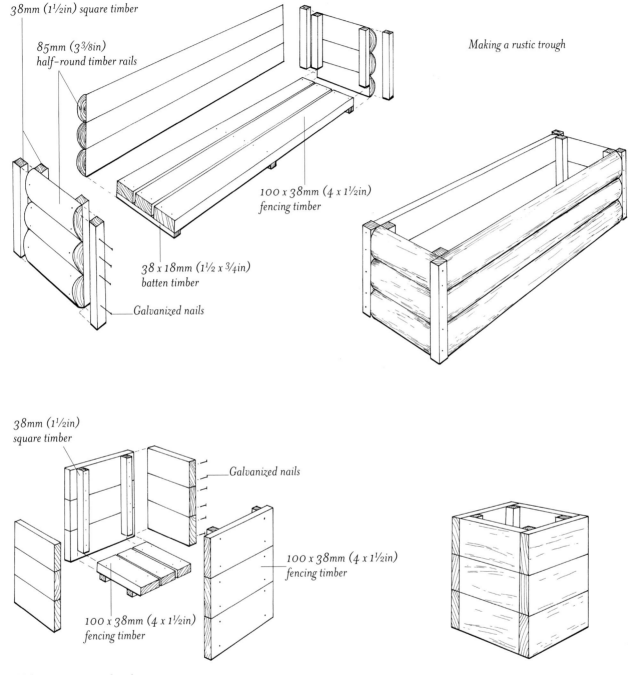

38mm (1½in) square timber

85mm (3⅜in) half-round timber rails

Making a rustic trough

100 x 38mm (4 x 1½in) fencing timber

38 x 18mm (1½ x ¾in) batten timber

Galvanized nails

38mm (1½in) square timber

Galvanized nails

100 x 38mm (4 x 1½in) fencing timber

100 x 38mm (4 x 1½in) fencing timber

Making a square wooden planter

Before an old container is used for plants you should clean it thoroughly. Use a stiff brush to remove as much dirt as possible, then scrub thoroughly with detergent and hot water and rinse clean with plenty of cold water. Many containers are then ready for use in their natural state. Some, particularly old metal containers, may benefit from a rust-inhibiting coat of paint or other decorative coating. A wide selection of suitable products is available from any good do-it-yourself store.

BASES AND SUPPORTS

Many containers need to be raised off the ground to improve drainage. Careful choice of supports will ensure that they blend with the container and enhance rather than detract from it.

Sinks and troughs will often look more attractive if raised several inches from the ground. Bricks are a popular choice, and can be built up two or three layers high if required. Softer types are ideal, as they are likely to weather more quickly. Concrete blocks can also be used to provide simple supports for sinks, but these are quite stark and therefore need to be hidden by careful planting at their base, or by placing smaller containers in a group around them.

Raising pots and similar containers 1–2cm (¹/₂–1in) above the surface will provide for extra-good drainage, and pot feet can be bought specifically for this purpose. These usually come as a set of three little terracotta 'feet' that are placed evenly around the base of the pot to raise it up. Small tiles or similar hard, flat material can be used. Containers standing on gravel should be able to drain freely without needing to be raised.

Terracotta containers that stand on a hard surface can be raised slightly on a piece of wood in winter to stop them freezing to the surface. We have found this precaution effective for old terracotta pots as well as modern ones.

Composts

GENERAL ADVICE

Good compost is one of the major keys to success with container gardening. Composts for containers need to be free-draining to prevent waterlogging in winter, but capable of holding enough water in the summer to prevent excessive drying out between watering times. As the only source of nutrients for a container plant, composts need to have a good initial content of fertilizer, and then be able to hold on to any fertilizer that is applied over subsequent seasons.

To provide the required drainage, the compost must contain open, fibrous material, which must remain stable and not break down and 'close up' the compost. After some time the compost will become full of plant roots, which will reduce its ability to hold water and nutrients, causing plant growth to suffer. Before this stage is reached, the plants in the container should be moved into a larger container with some fresh compost.

COMPOST MIXES

Peat-based compost alone will dry out too quickly and lose its structure when used for long-term plantings, whereas John Innes compost, which is soil-based, is very heavy on its own and tends to become rather solid. Together they provide a more open compost that will sustain a permanent planting with regular feeding.

A good general mix for containers in this book

⁓ 1 part peat-based compost
⁓ 1 part John Innes No 2

Decrease the amount of John Innes compost considerably for hanging baskets, or they will be too heavy.

An ideal mix for sinks, troughs and shallow containers

⁓ 1 part peat-based compost
⁓ 1 part John Innes No 2
⁓ 1 part flint grit

Increase the amount of peat-based compost for sink plantings of moist peat-loving plants, and increase the John Innes compost and grit when a more sharply drained compost is required.

A good mix for acid-loving plants

⁓ 1 part ericaceous peat-based compost
⁓ 1 part horticultural sand
(or acid loam if available)
For sinks and shallow containers add:
⁓ 1 part flint grit

PLANTING UP CONTAINERS

We have found that spending time preparing and planting a container properly will result in a long-lasting feature that will give many years of enjoyment.

Large pots and similar containers

1   Before starting to plant, make sure that all the plants you are going to use are moist. Soak any that are dry for at least an hour, in a bucket of water up to the top of their compost.
2   Place heavy containers in their final position before you begin to plant.
3   Cover the drainage holes with a few broken crocks or large stones, and then add a generous layer of drainage material, such as pea shingle, to a depth of 5–10cm (2–4in) if the height of the container allows.
4   Fill the container to within 8cm (3in or so) of the top with your chosen compost mix, without any firming down. To save compost in very deep containers such as chimney pots, it is a good idea to include a layer of old potting compost or good garden soil in the bottom before adding about 30cm (12in) of new compost on top.
5   Before you begin planting, we suggest you experiment with different arrangements of your plants while they are still in their pots.
6   When you are happy with the arrangement, begin planting one plant at a time. Carefully remove the plant from its pot and, using a trowel, dig a hole slightly bigger than the size of the root ball; then place it in the hole and gently firm some compost around the roots.
7   When all the plants are in place, add further compost if necessary to bring the level up to about 3cm (1in or so) below the top of the container.
8   After planting, water the container thoroughly in order to firm the compost around the plants and settle everything in.

PLANTING UP SINKS AND TROUGHS

The method is similar, but as sinks are very heavy it is essential that they are placed in their final position before they are planted. Before adding compost to the sink, cover the drainage hole inside with a piece of zinc gauze (available from hardware shops), which helps to keep out some pests and also stops compost falling through. A good layer of drainage material should then be added in the base. Broken crocks or pea shingle are ideal for this, and should be added to a depth of 3–4cm (1¼–1½in) in all but the shallowest sinks.

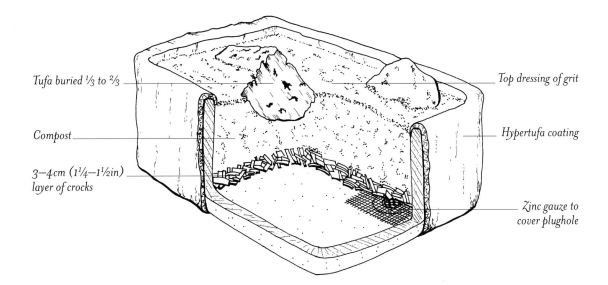

Tufa buried ⅓ to ⅔

Compost

3–4cm (1¼–1½in) layer of crocks

Top dressing of grit

Hypertufa coating

Zinc gauze to cover plughole

Preparing a sink for planting

It is difficult to include a layer of drainage material in a very shallow trough, so add some extra grit to the compost instead, so that it can drain freely. If pieces of rock or tufa are going to be included they should be buried one- to two-thirds below the surface of the compost before planting commences.

TOP-DRESSING CONTAINERS

Top-dressing the compost is a good finishing touch. As well as reducing weed growth, it helps to prevent moisture loss. You don't have to top-dress small pots – the foliage of many plants will cover the surface sufficiently anyway. Sinks and troughs, however, do look better with a top dressing.

Use grit on sinks and other containers with small plants such as alpines and sempervivums; it looks attractive, as well as improving the drainage at the base of the plants. Ericaceous and woodland-type plantings in sinks are best mulched with a very fine bark instead.

For larger containers, gravel or fine bark can be used, according to preference. The only problem with bark is that birds will spread it around in their search for insects. However, it does look attractive as a mulch for shrubs, conifers, heathers and perennials that like

A top dressing of flint grit looks attractive on containers; it is ideal around this lavender, as it also improves the sharp drainage at the plant's base

moisture-retentive compost. Use grit or gravel for silver plants and others that need sharp drainage – if you use bark on these, the bases of the plants will stay too damp and may start to rot.

REFRESHING ESTABLISHED CONTAINERS

For long-established plants, you should scrape away the top layer of compost and replace with fresh compost. Do this at least once a year, but preferably twice, in spring and autumn.

REPLANTING ESTABLISHED CONTAINERS

After a time, plants in containers can begin to look tired and lack the vigour and gloss they once had. If the container has also become very slow to take up water, then the compost has probably broken down and become solid, or it is completely full of roots. When a container reaches this stage it is time to replant and refresh the compost.

To remedy this situation, we recommend the following course of action if you want to re-use the same container:

For an individual plant in a container

1 Remove the plant from the container.
2 Gently tease any compost away from the roots.
3 Using a hand fork, scrape as much compost away as possible.
4 If necessary, cut away areas of matted root until the root ball has been reduced enough to allow a good layer of fresh compost to be placed all around it in the pot. New, fresh roots will soon grow out. Alternatively, leave out this stage and replant using a larger pot with fresh compost.

For a mixed container

1 Remove the planting from the container.
2 Remove any compost from around the edge.
3 Carefully pull the plants apart. It often helps to cut the compost gently with an old knife. Most fibrous-rooted plants will benefit from having their roots trimmed in this way. Take care, however, to minimize damage to any bulbs and the crowns of dormant plants, and don't cut through tap-rooted plants (plants with one long, thick root).

4 You can then replant into new compost in a larger container. If the original container is being re-used, leave one or more of the original plants out to provide more room and compost for the others to develop, or divide up some of the plants where possible to make smaller clumps.

WATERING

Plants in containers need regular watering. The compost should be kept constantly moist to the touch, particularly during the hot summer months. Plants with large or lush foliage, or containers packed with plants, will need more watering than alpines and evergreens in general. Pots in sunny positions will dry out more than those in shady spots. Containers with sharp or good drainage will dry out more than those with moisture-retentive compost, but will require less water in general. Compost mixes which combine both soil-based and peat-based compost are less prone to complete drying out than peat-based compost alone.

Established sinks, unless they are very shallow, should only need watering during long dry spells in summer. Water newly planted sinks thoroughly once a week or so, except after rain, until established. The types of plants grown in sinks don't tend to require vast amounts of water, but they must not be allowed to dry out.

For those with limited time there is a vast range of automatic watering equipment available, which can be set up to provide water for containers. With careful planning, systems can be laid out so they are nearly invisible. They can be controlled manually or, by using electronic timers, the system can operate during holidays and other periods of absence.

FEEDING

The compost mixes we have suggested should provide enough nutrients for several weeks' initial growth, after which regular feeding will be required.

For larger containers we often incorporate a slow-release fertilizer into the mix. Depending on the brand, this will give up to 12 months of feed. Even with this included, we find that the plants can benefit from an additional feed when they begin to grow rapidly in the spring. There is a wide range of feeds available, all of which are effective if used according to the manufacturer's instructions. In general, solid fertilizers are ideal for those of you with limited time; they tend to last longer than liquid feeds, which need to be applied frequently in the growing season.

Solid fertilizer, particularly the slow-release type, is more effective if gently incorporated into the surface of the compost, where it remains moist and can steadily release the nutrients. Left on the surface, it is effective only when it rains or when the container is watered.

Sink and trough plantings should be fed sparingly only once a year, ideally in the spring, using a slow-release fertilizer. You will want the plants to remain compact and true to form, and overfeeding will cause excess lush growth. Take particular care to prevent the fertilizer coming into contact with the foliage of small alpines, otherwise severe scorching can occur.

Using tufa

You can use pieces of rock in some containers to add structure and height, most appropriately in sinks and pans. Of all the types of rock available to gardeners, tufa is one of the most versatile, particularly for container gardening. Tufa is a natural water-formed rock, being a form of limestone. It is very light, with a highly porous structure, so that it is easily broken and is soft enough to allow plants to grow into the rock itself. You can make holes in it, and can sometimes find natural pockets in its surface to put little plants into. Tufa is like a sponge, soaking up water and drying out rapidly. To keep it moist enough to grow plants in successfully, it needs to be buried about one-third into the compost so that it can soak up sufficient water.

Tufa is soft enough to be broken roughly where necessary. This allows pieces suitable for containers to be cut with ease to the approximate shape and size required. We usually break ours with a wide brick bolster and lump hammer, which gives reasonably good control of where the break occurs. Any small pieces that are produced can be used in pans and sinks to provide added structure. The cut surfaces of the tufa will rapidly develop a weathered appearance, particularly over the autumn and winter months. Initially a creamy-white colour, it weathers to a light grey and soon develops mossy patches.

PLANTING A TUFA CLIFF

You can create your own miniature tufa cliff in a pan, to grow some choice alpines in.

1 Select a piece of tufa soft enough to bore holes in with a blunt screwdriver. Choose a container large enough to take the piece of tufa and deep enough so that about one-third of the tufa can be buried. Pans, low bowls and troughs are ideal, or you can use several pieces in a sink. Fill your container with the appropriate compost mix suggested previously.

2 Using your screwdriver, bore holes about 3cm (1¹/4in) in diameter and 4.5cm (1³/4in) deep in the tufa, scraping away at the tufa until you have made

a decent hole. Make as many holes as you require, then bury the tufa about one-third deep in the compost in your container.

3 To establish well, the plants used need to be young and growing vigorously. If they have been grown as plug plants, they can simply be pushed into the pockets in the tufa. Seedlings are also easy to establish, provided care is taken to fill the pocket completely with compost. Pot-grown plants may need to have their root balls carefully reduced by teasing away the compost and trimming excess roots; loose roots should not be twisted and squashed into the base of the pockets. Once the plants are in their pockets, dry compost should be carefully trickled in around them and firmed gently

Make holes in the tufa by scraping away with a blunt screwdriver, then set the tufa piece into a container and fill around with compost

Place the plant into the hole, pushing the roots well in. Trickle compost around the plant and push gently in

Once the tufa is planted up, finish with a layer of grit around the container

Water carefully by trickling water slowly from a can, until both the tufa and the compost in the container are moistened

with a blunt, narrow instrument to ensure that no air pockets are left. Soil-based compost such as John Innes is best for this.

4 After planting, the pockets need to be watered carefully to settle the plants and compost. The compost in the container should also be thoroughly watered. Finish with a top dressing of grit around the container.

5 While the plants are establishing, both the pockets and the container should be watered regularly, but once they are settled, the tufa will draw water up from the container, as long as this is kept well watered.

USING TUFA IN SINKS

You can use tufa in sinks and pans for structure and interest, in the same way that you would use other pieces of rock. Tufa is easier to position than other kinds, as it has no definite strata. Two or three pieces added to a sink before planting create extra height, as well as a cool root run for some of the plants. You can increase the depth of compost in shallow sinks by building it up between pieces of tufa. Remember to

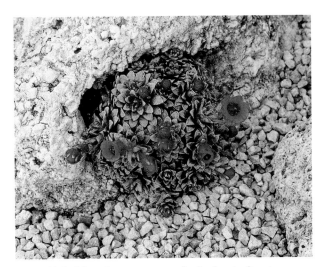

An established Saxifraga in a piece of tufa, showing limestone chippings used as a top dressing

bury each piece one- to two-thirds into the surface of the compost. You can also use planted pieces in your sink, establishing the plants as described above. Any plants placed near the tufa will gradually grow over and into it, blending it into your miniature landscape. Even tiny pieces can add character to a small pan of alpines.

7

Problems, pests and diseases

General and cultural problems

Plants in containers are far more susceptible to neglect than those in the open garden. Their roots are unable to spread out far in search of water and nutrients, so you need to provide these regularly, or your plants will soon show signs of stress and neglect.

DROUGHT

One of the most common problems with containers is lack of water. During the summer months plants grow rapidly and need to take up considerable amounts of water to make up for what they lose from the leaf surfaces. The most obvious sign of drought is wilting, but many plants, particularly woody ones, begin to suffer long before this. Often this can be seen in a lack of growth and a general lack of freshness in the foliage. Leaves will become curled and yellow with brown edges, and will begin to fall.

Drought problems can occur even in containers that are regularly watered. If an unsuitable compost is used, with no fibre to hold the moisture, water can often go straight through and out of the bottom of the pot. The same can also occur if the plants have filled the pot with roots, as the compost will no longer be able to hold any water.

In both cases the solution is to replant the container using a compost mix as described in Chapter 6. For pot-bound plants, replanting into a larger container is usually the best solution.

If your container has dried out because you have forgotten to water it, try standing it in a large tray or bucket filled with water so that the container is immersed as much as possible. Leave it to soak up the water, refilling the bucket as necessary, until the compost is moist again.

WATERLOGGING

Containers left outside during the winter months can become waterlogged very quickly if drainage is poor, either because of poorly aerated compost or because the drainage holes have become blocked by standing on a solid surface.

Typical symptoms include wilting and flagging leaves and yellowing of foliage. Soft leaves start turning mouldy, and this spreads to stems and flowers. Roots become soft, brown and rotten, as there is insufficient air in the compost to keep them healthy. Low-growing succulent plants such as *Sedum* and *Sempervivum* may well rot off at the base.

The solution is to improve the drainage, by changing the compost and raising the container off the surface, using pot feet or tiles as suggested in Chapter 6. Make sure you put plenty of crocks in the base of the container. More susceptible plants could be moved under cover during wet periods in winter, but if they have sharp drainage and are raised off the ground, there is no reason why they shouldn't survive.

ETIOLATED GROWTH

New stems and leaves may become drawn out, thin and pale; this is usually caused by a lack of light. Take care when positioning your containers. A container placed in winter sun may receive no light at all once the leaves on surrounding plants emerge again in spring. The plants in the container can then become very drawn as they try to grow towards the light.

Excessive feeding with a nitrogen-rich feed can sometimes cause similar problems. Take care to use only balanced feeds at the intervals and strengths recommended by the manufacturer.

LEAF SCORCH

Too much bright summer sun often causes browning of the leaves, particularly of yellow and variegated foliage. Containers of such plants should be positioned carefully, as areas of shade in autumn and winter can frequently get the full heat of the sun as it rises higher in the sky in the summer months. Plants with golden foliage are best placed out of the midday sun; put them where they will receive morning or afternoon sun only, as they do require *some* bright light to retain their golden colour.

Solid fertilizer remaining on the foliage can also cause leaf scorch, so if you use granular fertilizer, make sure you put it on the compost only, avoiding the foliage. Water droplets on leaves can cause sun scorch, so try to water your containers in the morning or evening rather than the middle of the day.

Pests and diseases

Aphids

A bad attack of aphids, or greenfly, can cause major damage to any planting, but conditions in containers are often particularly good for aphids, with fresh growth on closely packed plants in a reasonably sheltered position.

There are numerous types of aphids, with colours ranging from green through red to black, all of which will cause very similar damage. The first symptom of an attack is often a sticky coating on the young growth. At this stage the first aphids can be seen by a keen eye. This sticky secretion often becomes coated with a black, sooty mould, turning the leaf surface black and unsightly. This is often accompanied by small white debris on the leaves beneath, which are the skins shed by the rapidly developing aphids. If an attack is left unchecked, the new leaves can become distorted, resulting in reduced growth, and – in severe attacks on young plants – the death of the plants.

There are a large number of insecticides on the market which are effective against aphids. The best ones to use are those which are selective and not toxic to beneficial insects such as ladybirds and bees.

Biological control methods can be equally effective. In the early stages of an attack, gently washing the shoot tips with soapy water will greatly reduce the aphid numbers, and this procedure repeated several times over a few weeks may be all that is required. For more established colonies, a regular spray with soft

A colony of aphids on the shoot tips of a **Hebe**

soap will reduce the problem and help to lessen the stickiness on the leaves.

Infestations occurring later in the year, in particular, often get cleared up by other insects that attack the aphids, such as ladybirds and hoverflies, so unless an attack is severe, leave nature to take its course.

ROOT APHIDS

Root aphids can frequently be found in containers, but are only visible when the plants are removed from the pot. They appear around the edges as white specks of a powdery substance which, on examination, each contain a small aphid. In established plants they rarely have a significant effect on growth; usually only young seedlings are severely affected.

Control is difficult, although limited success can sometimes be achieved by watering the compost with a spray-strength solution of an insecticide recommended for leaf and shoot aphids.

VINE WEEVILS

Vine weevil infestation can cause devastation in a container. If you find your plants wilting and looking stunted in early to mid-spring, and drought is obviously not a cause, then vine weevil larvae are the likely culprits. They are white legless grubs about 1cm

Vine weevil larvae are distinctive, with a curved white body and a brown head

(3/8in) long, with distinctive brown heads. If the plants are removed from the container, the larvae can be found just below the surface of the compost where they chew the roots. If left unchecked they will eventually separate the plant from its root system – hence the wilting of foliage, flowers and stems.

Control of the larvae with insecticides can be difficult. Short-term control is possible with special insecticide-treated compost, but this is only effective for the first six months.

The most effective treatment is to use biological control, treating the compost with nematodes in mid-summer. To be effective, the nematodes must be watered onto warm, moist compost (above 12°C or 54°F), where they will seek out the vine weevil larvae, infect and kill them.

If the damage to plants is not too severe when it is first noticed, you can often save the plants. Carefully remove the original compost, destroying any larvae you find, and repot the plants in fresh compost. Feed and water them well to help them re-establish.

Adult vine weevils can also cause damage, although this tends to be cosmetic. It usually takes the form of small semicircular bites removed from the edges of leaves. While this does little damage to the plant itself, apart from aesthetic considerations, it does serve as a warning that the compost should be treated to prevent damage by the larvae.

SLUGS AND SNAILS

Slugs and snails have a voracious appetite for soft vegetable material, and the damage they cause ranges from holes in the edges and centre of leaves to the complete destruction of all top growth on perennials such as *Ajuga*, *Hosta*, *Campanula* and many others. Low-growing mats of succulent plants such as *Sedum* and *Sempervivum* can often be separated from their roots, as the slugs in particular will shelter under their protective cushions and eat away at the fleshy stems.

Slugs and snails can be readily controlled with the various brands of slug pellets, but non-chemical methods can be just as good. Sharp grit, used as a top dressing, is unpleasant to the soft bodies of slugs and is a good deterrent. In larger containers, it is possible to install slug traps baited with liquid such as beer. Slug pellets are effective in containers, where they are less of a risk to birds and pets than in the open garden, because they are less conspicuous in a limited area and are likely to be hidden by foliage. Just a few, sprinkled on the compost surface when the container is first planted, or in early spring as lush growth starts, can be enough. Put a few under a stone or a slightly raised tile, out of the reach of birds and animals but where the slugs and snails will still find them.

Treating the compost with nematodes that infect and kill the slugs is another effective method. The nematodes can be applied in the spring once the soil temperature rises above 5°C (40°F). They will remain active for up to six weeks if the compost is kept moist.

A longer-term control can be achieved by placing slug tape around each pot. This is a self-adhesive copper band, which slugs and snails will not cross, and will last on each container for several years.

MILDEW

Two types of mildew can occur in container-grown plants, namely downy mildew and powdery mildew. Downy mildew usually shows itself as discoloured areas on the upper part of the leaf with corresponding furry or downy grey patches beneath. Powdery mildew generally develops as a white powdery coating on the upper side of the leaf, which can then spread under the leaf and onto other parts of the plant. The exact symptoms vary from plant to plant and the two forms are often confused. Fortunately this is not a problem, as the treatments are very similar.

Downy mildew is particularly common in a moist environment and can be curtailed by ensuring good air movement around the containers and by not watering the foliage.

Powdery mildew tends to be a summer problem and occurs when plants are dry at the roots but have moisture around the foliage. Regular watering and good air movement, avoiding dank corners, will help prevent the problem.

With both types of mildew, infected leaves and stems should be trimmed back and destroyed. Proprietary fungicides can be used effectively if they are applied in the early stages of infection.

Chemical treatments from the garden centre containing mancozeb, carbendazin or sulphur can be effective against powdery mildew, and treatments based on mancozeb can offer control of downy mildew.

8

Planting plans

This chapter includes ten detailed designs for a variety of containers, each with a key for identification, a list of the plants used, and a description of the effect achieved. You can either follow the plan exactly as it is given, or use any of the suggested alternatives or adaptations. The designs contain one of each plant used, unless stated otherwise. The idea of these designs is to help you choose plants that associate well, so if you substitute plants of your own choice, try to keep the overall effect similar. The type of container used is described, together with its dimensions, but you can of course use anything similar, or a container of your choice.

Plan 1

CONTAINER
30cm (12in)
terracotta pot with
basket-weave effect

COMPOST
Sharply drained
compost with a top
dressing of grit

POSITION
Full sun

PLANTS

1 *Lavandula angustifolia* 'Imperial Gem'

2 *Hyssopus officinalis* subsp. *aristatus*

3 *Helianthemum* 'Ben Ledi'

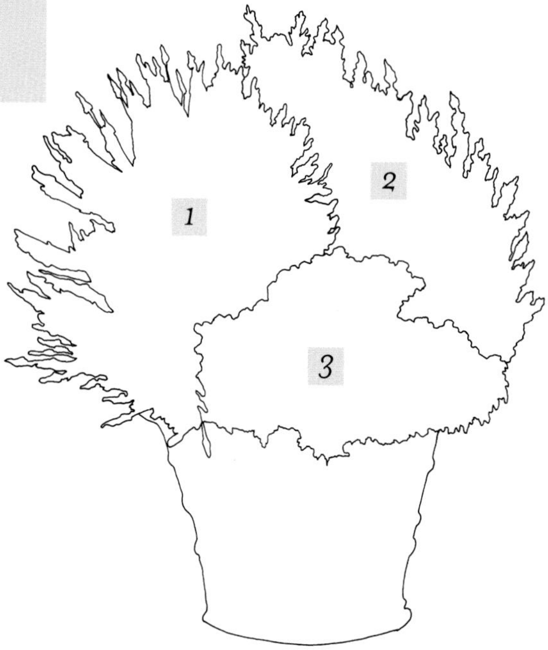

This is a container planting featuring aromatic foliage and masses of colourful flowers all summer long. Silvery-green and deep green bushy dwarf shrubs carry deep blue and dark violet spikes together with rich, rose-red, rounded blooms, all revelling in a hot sunny spot. This is a particularly lovely arrangement for a basket-weave-effect terracotta pot – or you could use a deep blue glazed container. Prune all the plants back quite hard after flowering to promote fresh bushy growth; this will often produce a second flowering on the *Helianthemum*.

Alternatives

1 Use any rosy red, pink or white *Helianthemum*, for example 'Wisley White' or the pink 'Sudbury Gem'.

2 Replace the *Helianthemum* with the stunning white crimson-centred flowers of *Cistus* x *dansereaui* 'Decumbens'.

Plan 2

CONTAINER
28cm (11in)
diameter pot, either
matt blue or green

COMPOST
Well drained, with a
top dressing of grit

POSITION
Sun

PLANTS

1 *Sisyrinchium striatum*
2 *Alchemilla mollis*
3 *Coreopsis verticillata*

A striking arrangement showing a sharp
contrast of leaf shape and texture,
together with toning flower colours, in
an attractive pot with muted colouring.
Smooth, linear, iris-like leaves contrast
with soft, rounded, greyish-green,
velvety leaves and finely divided, dark
green, ferny foliage. Yellow starry daisies,
pale yellow spires and tiny creamy-green
blooms cover the plants for a long
period throughout the summer.

Alternatives

1 Replace the *Sisyrinchium* with *Iris
   pallida* 'Variegata', which has linear
   leaves striped with blue-green and
   primrose yellow, and pale mauve
   flowers.

2 For a different colour scheme with
   interesting foliage, use *Phormium*
   'Sundowner', *Sedum* 'Ruby Glow'
   and *Ballota pseudodictamnus*.
   Sword-like grey and pink foliage
   contrasts with fleshy, purple-tinged
   leaves on trailing stems and soft,
   felted, greyish-green round leaves,
   the deep rose-pink starry flowers of
   the *Sedum* adding bright colour in
   late summer.

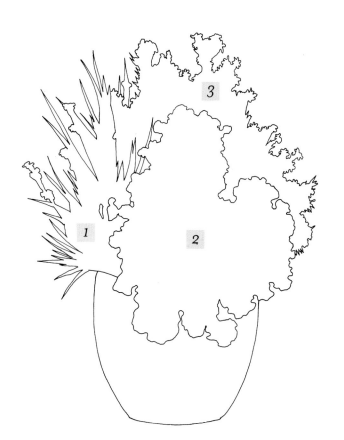

Plan 3

CONTAINER
38cm (15in)
diameter
earthenware pot

COMPOST
General compost
mix with a top
dressing of grit

POSITION
Sun

PLANTS

1   *Santolina* 'Lambrook Silver'

2   *Berberis thunbergii* 'Dart's Red Lady'

3   *Salvia* x *sylvestris* 'Blauhügel'

A stunning contrast between the deep purple-red *Berberis* and bright silver *Santolina* is highlighted further by the matt-textured leaves and light blue spikes of *Salvia*. In this design, the overall plant shapes as well as leaf colour, shape and texture play an important part. The fresh new growth in spring, the foliage colour and flowers in summer, and the rich autumn tints of the *Berberis* give this planting a long season of interest. A plain earthenware pot in a neutral shade is all that is needed.

Alternative

1   Replace the *Santolina* and *Salvia* with *Campanula poscharskyana* and *Carex morrowii* 'Evergold' to give a completely different colour scheme of mauve and gold with the red *Berberis*.

Plan 4

CONTAINER
61 x 46cm (24 x 18in) stone sink, or hypertufa-covered porcelain sink

COMPOST
Well drained, gritty compost with a top dressing of fine grit

POSITION
Sun

PLANTS

1	Hebe 'Colwall'
2	Aquilegia flabellata 'Ministar'
3	Juniperus communis 'Compressa'
4	Phlox douglasii 'Crackerjack'
5	Dianthus 'Nyewoods Cream'
6	Alyssum spinosum 'Roseum'
7	Silene acaulis 'Mount Snowdon'
8	Thymus serpyllum 'Minimus'
9	Ilex crenata 'Mariesii'
10	Sisyrinchium idahoense
11	Geranium dalmaticum
12	Minuartia stellata
13	Sempervivum arachnoideum
14	Veronica prostrata 'Nana'

A mixed landscape planting, with a miniature conifer and two dwarf evergreen shrubs to provide height and structure. A selection of cushion, tufted and rosette alpines have been chosen for their habit, foliage and flower to give variety and a long flowering season. Trailing alpines cover the edges and corners of the sink, and a tufa rock outcrop provides crevices for planting tiny alpines into. The plants will flower from early spring until late summer, in colours of blue, pink, white and cream. Leaf shapes are varied, including linear, rounded, needle-like and spiky, in all shades of green with some silver and red.

Alternatives

1 Use any miniature conifer instead of the *Juniperus*, for example *Cryptomeria japonica* 'Compressa' or *Chamaecyparis lawsoniana* 'Gnome'.
2 Replace the small holly (*Ilex*) with the dwarf gnarled willow *Salix* 'Boydii' or the miniature cotton lavender *Santolina chamaecyparissus* 'Small-Ness'.
3 Use any tiny *Phlox*, *Dianthus* or *Sempervivum* in place of those suggested.

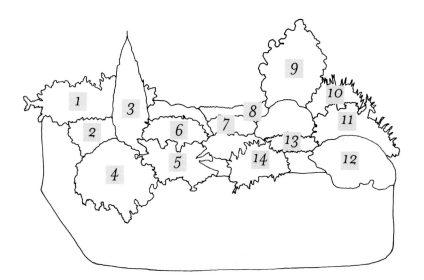

Plan 5

CONTAINER
Stone trough with minimal decoration, 60 x 25cm (24 x 10in) with a depth of 20–25cm (8–10in).

COMPOST
Well drained, with a top dressing of grit

POSITION
Sun

PLANTS

1   *Dianthus* 'Doris'

2   *Sedum spectabile* 'Brilliant'

3   *Festuca glauca* 'Blaufuchs'

4   *Allium cernuum* x 3

5   *Gypsophila repens* (white) x 2

A gentle pastel scheme providing contrasting foliage and a long season of flower colour. The rounded, succulent leaves of *Sedum* and the tiny foliage of the trailing *Gypsophila* are a similar pale green, while the *Dianthus* and *Festuca* both make silvery-blue mounds and the leaves of the *Allium* form a linear contrast. White, mauve, shrimp pink and bright pink blooms are borne from early summer and into autumn, with a contrast in scale and shape.

Alternatives

1   Use any border pink (*Dianthus*) with silver foliage and any small silvery-blue grass instead of those suggested.

2   Use ornamental herbs for a golden and green planting scheme, choosing variegated sage and lemon balm, chives, golden thyme and marjoram. These will give you a succession of white and mauve flowers during the summer, as well as edible leaves.

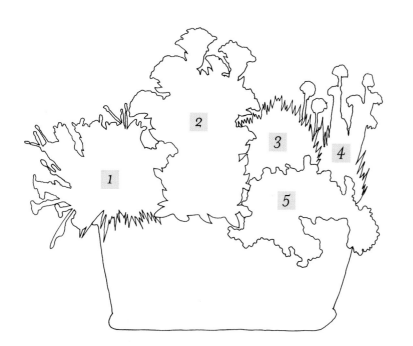

Plan 6

CONTAINER
Low, wide, shallow bowl-shaped container, 48cm (19in) in diameter

COMPOST
Moisture-retentive, with a top dressing of fine bark

POSITION
Partial shade

PLANTS

1   *Hosta* 'Halcyon'

2   *Heuchera* 'Pewter Moon'

3   *Ophiopogon planiscapus* 'Nigrescens'

4   *Saxifraga* x *urbium*

An excellent foliage planting for a partially shady site, ideal for a wide container which will allow plenty of room for the leaves to display to advantage. The large, bold blue leaves of *Hosta* and deep purple-black grassy foliage of *Ophiopogon* contrast with the bright green *Saxifraga* and the *Heuchera* with its silvery-grey, maroon-backed leaves. Two of the plants bear masses of dainty flowers in summer. This container is at its best from early spring to late summer.

Alternatives

1   Replace the *Ophiopogon* with a small variegated sedge (*Carex*).

2   Choose any *Heuchera* with decorative foliage instead of the one suggested.

3   Replace the *Heuchera* with the ferny foliage and dainty pink flowers of *Dicentra spectabilis*.

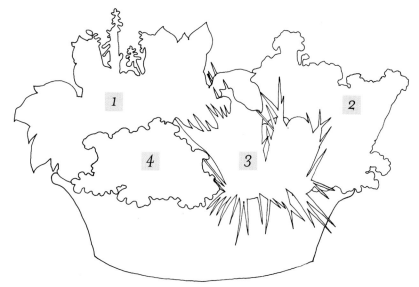

Plan 7

CONTAINER
46cm (18in)
diameter terracotta
container

COMPOST
Moisture-retentive,
with a top dressing
of fine bark

POSITION
Shade or partial
shade

PLANTS

1 *Dicentra spectabilis* 'Alba'

2 *Brunnera macrophylla*

3 *Helleborus* x *sternii*

4 *Primula* 'Garryard Guinevere'

5 *Anemone sylvestris* x 3

6 *Pulmonaria saccharata* 'Argentea'

7 *Heuchera micrantha* var.
   diversifolia 'Palace Purple'

A mixed perennial planting to give you a display for much of the year, with a variety of interesting foliage and a range of different flowers providing effect from winter through to summer. Bold, textured leaves, delicate ferny foliage, and frosted silver and deep purple leaves form a background tapestry to the dainty blue and white flower sprays. More substantial white, pink and pinkish-green blooms add further colour and interest. A large, deep terracotta pot holds sufficient compost to sustain this number of plants.

Alternatives

1 Use any white, pink or blue primula, with either single or double flowers.

2 Replace the *Brunnera* with a blue *Hosta*.

3 Replace the *Anemone* with a shade-loving *Geranium* such as *G. nodosum* or *G. phaeum*.

Plan 8

CONTAINER
Wooden window
box, 75 x 25cm
(30 x 10in) with a
depth of 23cm (9in)

COMPOST
General compost,
with no top
dressing

POSITION
Sun

PLANTS

1   *Erica carnea* 'Springwood White'

2   *Festuca glauca* 'Blaufuchs'

3   *Hebe vernicosa*

4   *Hedera helix* 'Adam'

5   *Euonymus fortunei* 'Golden Pillar'

6   *Sedum kamtschaticum* var.
floriferum 'Weihenstephaner Gold'

7   *Helianthemum* 'Wisley Primrose'

8   *Thymus* x *citriodorus* 'Archer's Gold'

9   *Narcissus* 'Tête-à-Tête' x 15
(not illustrated) to add colour
in spring

A golden and soft yellow scheme with touches of silvery-blue, pale lilac and white. This is a planting for year-round interest, with plenty of evergreens, a variety of foliage and plant shapes, and trailing plants to cascade down the front of the box. The planting includes a winter-flowering heather, spring-flowering dwarf narcissi, variegated and golden foliage, a small blue grass and colourful summer flowers. If you use a wooden window box, it could be stained or have a suitably coloured woodwash applied.

Alternatives

1   Use dwarf yellow or white tulips or crocuses instead of narcissi.

2   Add yellow or white primroses or mauve violas for more spring colour.

3   Replace the *Euonymus* or *Hebe* with a dwarf conifer.

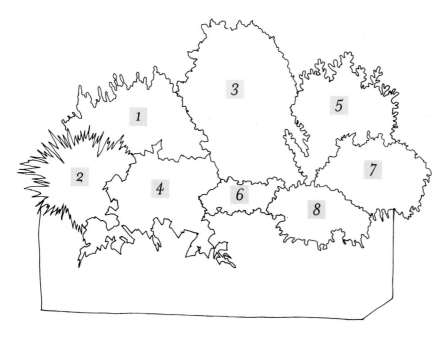

Plan 9

CONTAINER
38cm (15in)
diameter moss-
lined wire-mesh
hanging basket

COMPOST
General compost,
largely peat-based,
with no top
dressing

POSITION
Sun

PLANTS

1   *Anthemis punctata* subsp. *cupaniana*

2   *Ajuga reptans* 'Braunherz'

3   *Thymus herba-barona* x 3

4   *Geranium sanguineum* var. *striatum*

5   *Parahebe catarractae* 'Delight'

6   *Ophiopogon planiscapus* 'Nigrescens' x 2

A basket of perennials designed for foliage effect and a long flowering season. Silver, deep purple and green foliage provide year-round colour, forming trailing mounds, with blue, white, pale pink and reddish-pink flowers from mid-spring right through until late autumn. Much of the foliage is more or less evergreen. Refresh the top layer of compost in early spring ready for the next season's display, and make sure the basket does not dry out, as it contains mostly peat-based compost.

Alternatives

1   Add a few dwarf tulips or narcissi for early spring colour.

2   Use bushy and trailing alpines, with a similar colour scheme, for a smaller basket. Choose *Dianthus, Veronica, Gypsophila, Saponaria, Campanula* and *Thymus*.

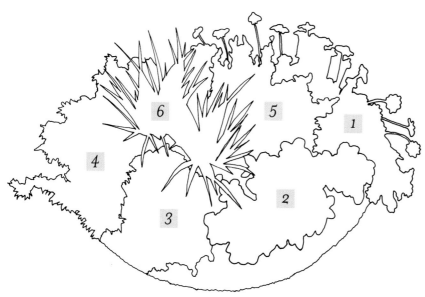

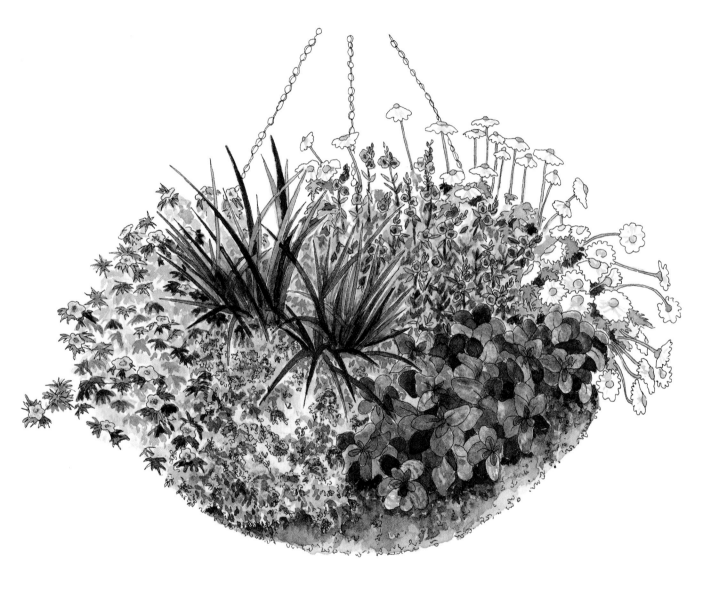

Plan 10

CONTAINER
60cm (24in)
diameter half-barrel
or 50cm (20in)
rustic tub

COMPOST
General compost
with a top dressing
of fine bark or
gravel

POSITION
Sun or light
dappled shade

PLANTS

1 *Hydrangea paniculata* 'Kyushu'

2 *Euonymus fortunei* 'Emerald Gaiety'

3 *Geranium wallichianum* 'Buxton's Variety'

4 *Vinca minor* 'Alba Variegata'

5 *Carex morrowii* 'Fisher's Form'

6 *Campanula* 'Elizabeth'

7 *Crocosmia* 'Severn Sunrise'

8 *Euphorbia amygdaloides* 'Rubra'

A substantial planting of shrubs and perennials for all-year-round interest, including plenty of evergreen foliage with variegated and tinted leaves on some of the plants. An upright, deciduous, late-flowering shrub is surrounded by a variety of foliage shapes, textures and colours, including sword-like leaves, glossy and rough-textured leaves, and striped, grassy foliage. The design includes bushy, rounded, arching, erect, trailing and scrambling plants, some intermingling, and some trailing over the sides, to form a densely planted tub. The colour scheme is mainly cream, white, plum pink and blue, with a little bright yellow-green and pinkish-orange.

Alternatives

1 Replace the *Hydrangea* with *Viburnum opulus* 'Nanum' or a small *Acer*.

2 Replace the *Vinca* with *Lamium maculatum* 'Beacon Silver', with its silvery-white leaves and pink flowers.

3 Add dwarf white or scarlet tulips for a splash of spring colour, and remove the bulbs when they have finished.

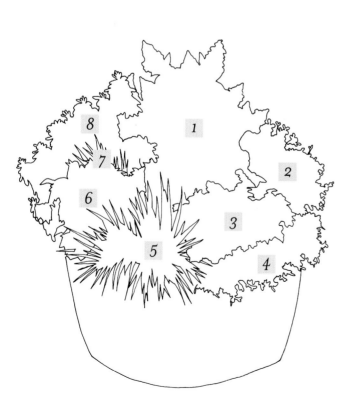

Plant descriptions

Many of the plants mentioned throughout this book are described more fully in this chapter, together with further examples where appropriate. This is not an exhaustive list by any means, but includes several examples of each category of hardy plant discussed.

The categories are indicated as follows:
A = alpine, **B** = bulb, **P** = perennial, **S** = shrub.
Grasses and sedges, conifers and ferns are listed separately at the end. For each plant, we have also indicated the position they prefer (sun, shade), the type of compost that suits them (moisture-retentive, ordinary, good or sharp drainage), and the flowering season (if any).

ACHILLEA

A ☼ ⊔	SPRING	SUMMER	AUTUMN	WINTER

The smaller alpine types, with ferny foliage and flat heads composed of many small flowers, are excellent for containers. *Achillea* 'Huteri' (8cm/3in) makes a neat hummock of aromatic, deeply cut grey foliage, with pure white flowers, while *A.* x *lewisii* 'King Edward' (10cm/4in) has more greyish-green leaves and soft lemon-yellow flowers.

AJUGA

P ☼ ● ▣	SPRING	SUMMER	AUTUMN	WINTER

Good ground-cover perennials, forming carpets of glossy leaves. In containers they will trail over the sides

Ajuga reptans 'Braunherz'

A = alpine   **B** = bulb   **P** = perennial   **S** = shrub   ☼ sun   ☼ semi-shade   ● shade

Alyssum spinosum 'Roseum'

and form mats underneath larger plants, or mingle with other foliage, creating a tapestry. Numerous dense spikes of flowers are borne on 10cm (4in) stems in late spring, giving a colourful show. *Ajuga reptans* 'Braunherz' has shining, bronzed, purple leaves with deep blue flowers, forming an effective colour contrast. 'Burgundy Glow' has smaller leaves variegated pink and cream, with paler blue flowers, and 'Pink Elf' has pink spikes above neat green foliage.

ALCHEMILLA *mollis*

| P ☀ ☼ ⊔ | SPRING | SUMMER | AUTUMN | WINTER |

Rounded leaves with a velvety texture, the crinkled edges holding water droplets after rain, and frothy sprays of tiny creamy-green flowers. Its lax habit makes it ideal for containers and baskets. 30-45cm (12–18in).

ALLIUM

| B ☀ ⊔ | SPRING | SUMMER | AUTUMN | WINTER |

Dainty to majestic varieties suitable for sinks, small and large containers. Flower heads composed of many individual flowers in a spherical or globular shape, usually mauve, pink or white. *A. cernuum* (23–30cm/ 9–12in) has graceful nodding heads of rose-purple.

A. beesianum (15cm/6in) is a tiny form with distinctive drooping heads of china blue. *A.* 'Lucy Ball' (90cm/3ft) has enormous round dark lilac flower heads on tall, straight stems.

ALYSSUM

| A ☀ ⊔ | SPRING | SUMMER | AUTUMN | WINTER |

Tiny shrublets with silvery-grey foliage, ideal for sinks and pans. *A. spinosum* 'Roseum' (10cm/4in) is a dense, spiny bush with many heads of soft rose-pink flowers, while *A. serpyllifolium* (10cm/4in) has golden-yellow flowers on trailing stems.

ANEMONE

| P/B ☀ ● ⊟ | SPRING | SUMMER | AUTUMN | WINTER |

A. sylvestris, the snowdrop anemone, produces mounds of deeply cut foliage and fragrant, slightly drooping white flowers on 30cm (12in) stems in mid-spring. It associates well with other perennials in a cool position.

Tuberous anemones (which are classed alongside bulbs in nurseries and catalogues) can be used for spring colour. The low-growing *A. blanda* has starry flowers in blue shades, pink or white, and can be grown with other bulbs or as a carpet in other plantings. *A. coronaria* has large black-centred flowers on strong

Anemone blanda

⊟ moisture-retentive   ⊟ ordinary drainage   ⊔ good drainage   ⊔ sharp drainage   ▮ ▮ ▮ flowering season

Anemone coronaria 'Mister Fokker'

20–30cm (8–12in) stems, borne in late spring and summer above ferny leaves; 'Mister Fokker' is a deep velvety purple, while 'The Admiral' has pink semi-double blooms.

ANTHEMIS *punctata* subsp. *cupaniana*

| P ☀ ⊔ | | SPRING | SUMMER | AUTUMN | WINTER |

Spreading, mounded plant up to 30cm (12in) with silvery-green cut foliage and a long succession of pure white daisy-like flowers with yellow centres. Cut back in late summer.

ARTEMISIA

| P ☀ ⊔ | | SPRING | SUMMER | AUTUMN | WINTER |

Wonderful silver foliage plants, including *A. absinthium* 'Lambrook Silver' (75cm/30in) with silky, aromatic, silvery-grey foliage and greyish flowers. *A. ludoviciana* 'Silver Queen' has more delicate silvery divided leaves. They are best cut down in late spring to allow new fresh growth, and all require a warm, sunny spot.

ASTER *novi-belgii*

| P ☀ ⊡ | | SPRING | SUMMER | AUTUMN | WINTER |

These bushy dwarf forms, of which there are many named varieties, have clumps of dark green foliage and many stems of rayed flowers in autumn. They vary in height from 25 to 35cm (10–14in). 'Kristina' is pure white, 'Lady in Blue' has semi-double rich blue flowers, and 'Little Pink Beauty' is soft pink.

AUCUBA *japonica*

| S ● ☼ ⊡ | | SPRING | SUMMER | AUTUMN | WINTER |

Dense, rounded evergreen shrub (1.5m/5ft) with large, glossy, leathery leaves. 'Variegata' has leaves speckled with yellow, 'Picturata' has leaves with a deep green margin and gold centre, while 'Golden King' is boldly speckled with gold.

BALLOTA *pseudodictamnus*

| P ☀ ⊔ | | SPRING | SUMMER | AUTUMN | WINTER |

A shrubby mound of woolly stems, up to 40cm (16in), clothed in felted grey-green rounded leaves. Whorls of tiny pink flowers with enlarged pale green calyces are carried in summer. This is a lovely plant for foliage effect, associating well with deeper colours, with pink flowers or with pastel shades.

BERBERIS

| S ☀ ☼ ⊡ | | SPRING | SUMMER | AUTUMN | WINTER |

A wide variety of forms suitable for containers, the evergreens valuable for glossy leaves and deciduous forms for brilliant autumn colour and bright berries. All have many yellow or orange flowers, and all are spiny. *B.* x *frikartii* 'Amstelveen' is a dense, arching evergreen, 80 x 80cm (32 x 32in), the glossy dark green leaves having blue-white undersides.

B. thunbergii is deciduous and has several dwarf forms. Globular-shaped bushes to 30–45cm (12–18in) include the slow-growing 'Aurea' with yellow leaves turning pale green in summer, 'Bagatelle' with crimson leaves, and 'Kobold' with green leaves colouring well in autumn. 'Dart's Red Lady' has a more spreading habit, to 60–90cm (2–3ft), with deepest purple leaves. The

---

A = alpine   B = bulb   P = perennial   S = shrub   ☀ sun   ☼ semi-shade   ● shade

1.5m (5ft) tall, stiff, upright stems of 'Erecta' are clothed in fresh green leaves, showing excellent fiery autumn colours.

BETULA *nana*

| S | ☀ | ▣ | | SPRING | SUMMER | AUTUMN | WINTER |

Slow-growing dwarf birch, up to 1m (3ft 3in), with tiny, neat leaves on thin spreading branches. Small yellow catkins emerge with the young leaves.

BRUNNERA *macrophylla*

| P | ● | ▣ | | SPRING | SUMMER | AUTUMN | WINTER |

Invaluable, forming robust clumps of large, rough-textured leaves and bearing many sprays of tiny bright blue flowers. Up to 45cm (18in).

BUXUS *sempervirens*

| S | ☀ | ● | ▣ | | SPRING | SUMMER | AUTUMN | WINTER |

The dwarf forms of box can be grown as specimens, and respond well to clipping, so various shapes can be achieved. 'Suffruticosa' (20cm/8in) has shiny green

Ceratostigma plumbaginoides

leaves, while 'Elegantissima' (40cm/16in) has green leaves irregularly margined creamy-white.

CAMPANULA

| A | ☀ | ◑ | ▣ | ▣ | | SPRING | SUMMER | AUTUMN | WINTER |

Alpine bellflowers are lovely in small containers or as an edging to larger plantings. *C. carpatica* 'Blaue Clips' (10cm/4in) has large upturned bell-shaped flowers of china blue on neat mounds, and *C. poscharskyana* 'Stella' forms larger mounds with long sprays of starry violet flowers. *C. cochleariifolia* 'Elizabeth Oliver', with tiny hanging double flowers of soft powder blue, is neat enough for a sink.

CENTAUREA *bella*

| P | ☀ | ⊔ | | SPRING | SUMMER | AUTUMN | WINTER |

Mounded plant, up to 20cm (8in), with neat silvery-grey cut leaves and delicate soft pink flowers.

CERATOSTIGMA

| S | ☀ | ⊔ | | SPRING | SUMMER | AUTUMN | WINTER |

Beautiful small shrubs for late flower and autumn leaf colour. *C. plumbaginoides* forms low 20cm (8in) clumps of oval green leaves, the clusters of deep blue flowers contrasting effectively with the rich red autumn tints of the foliage. *C. willmottianum* is more twiggy and upright, to 60cm (2ft), with sky-blue flowers, and requires a warm position.

CHOISYA *ternata*

| S | ☀ | ◑ | ⊔ | | SPRING | SUMMER | AUTUMN | WINTER |

Handsome, rounded evergreen bush with glossy, aromatic trefoil foliage and clusters of sweetly scented white flowers. Excellent specimen shrub for a sheltered spot out of the wind. Reaching up to 1.5m (5ft), it can be pruned back hard if necessary.

CISTUS

| S | ☀ | ⊔ | | SPRING | SUMMER | AUTUMN | WINTER |

Bushy evergreen shrubs with a long succession of rounded, showy flowers. Low forms suitable for containers include *C. x dansereaui* 'Decumbens'

▣ moisture-retentive   ▣ ordinary drainage   ⊔ good drainage   ⊔ sharp drainage | | | | flowering season

Cistus x *dansereaui* 'Decumbens'

(60cm/2ft), which has dark green wavy-edged leaves and large, stunning white flowers with a central crimson blotch, and *C.* 'Silver Pink' (80cm/32in), with grey-green leaves and clear silvery-pink, yellow-centred flowers.

CONVOLVULUS *cneorum*

| S | ☀ | ⊔ | | Spring | Summer | Autumn | Winter |

A choice floriferous dwarf shrub clothed in soft, silky, silvery leaves, the clusters of furled pink-flushed buds opening into funnel-shaped ivory-white flowers. Requiring warm conditions, it grows up to 50cm (20in). Old growth is best cut out in spring.

COREOPSIS *verticillata*

| P | ☀ | ⊔ | | Spring | Summer | Autumn | Winter |

Free-flowering perennial with bright green divided foliage and 60cm (2ft) wiry stems carrying rich yellow starry daisy flowers well above the leaves. The pale creamy-yellow form 'Moonbeam' is particularly lovely, and slightly shorter at 45cm (18in).

CORNUS

| S | ☀ | ◐ | ⊟ | | Spring | Summer | Autumn | Winter |

There is an attractive dwarf dogwood, reaching 35cm (14in), which is ideal for pots. *C. stolonifera* 'Kelseyi' has red-tinted leaves that deepen in colour as autumn approaches. Once they have fallen, the deep red young twigs and yellow older stems retain interest all winter.

COTONEASTER *procumbens*

| S | ☀ | ● | ⊟ | | Spring | Summer | Autumn | Winter |

A low, creeping evergreen form, spreading to 30cm (12in), with small polished deep green leaves, white flowers and red berries, excellent for underplanting in containers.

A = alpine   B = bulb   P = perennial   S = shrub   ☀ sun   ◐ semi-shade   ● shade

CROCOSMIA

P ☼ ☀ ⊔ | SPRING | SUMMER | AUTUMN | WINTER

Handsome sword-like leaves and tall branching stems of 50-60cm (20–24in), each carrying several flowers in shades of orange, red and yellow in late summer. 'Emberglow' has red flowers, while 'Severn Sunrise' has blooms of an unusual light orange, flushed pink. *C. x crocosmiiflora* 'Solfaterre' carries pale apricot flowers above bronzed foliage, and 'Emily McKenzie' has wonderful large, flat star-shaped flowers, deep orange in colour with a mahogany-brown central blotch.

CROCUS

B ☼ ⊔ | SPRING | SUMMER | AUTUMN | WINTER

Funnel-shaped flowers in many shades of colour, opening out in the sun among narrow leaves with a white central stripe. Large-flowered ones include 'Pickwick', pearly-grey striped with lilac, and 'Remembrance' with deep purple blooms. Smaller *C. chrysanthus* types include 'Cream Beauty', which has creamy-yellow flowers with bright orange centres, and 'Blue Pearl', a soft shade of blue with paler blue inside.

CYCLAMEN

P ● ☀ ⊟ | SPRING | SUMMER | AUTUMN | WINTER

These hardy small cyclamen, up to 10cm (4in), are invaluable for planting around shrubs in pots, or in small perennial plantings. *C. coum* has rounded leaves, plain green or green marbled silver, and delightful stumpy little flowers in various shades of pink, stained maroon at the snout. It is winter-flowering, from mid-winter to mid-spring. *C. hederifolium* has dark green ivy-shaped foliage with silver and grey markings, and large pink flowers in autumn. There is also a white form, and a beautiful one called 'Nettleton Silver' with almost completely silvered leaves, forming a striking foliage contrast; this one has pink flowers.

DIANTHUS

A/P ☼ ⊔ | SPRING | SUMMER | AUTUMN | WINTER

Tiny alpine pinks suitable for sinks include 'Nyewoods Cream' (7cm/3in), a diminutive mound of grey-green leaves with fragrant cream flowers, and *D. erinaceus* (5cm/2in), a cushion of sharply pointed spiny leaves with rose-red flowers. A slightly larger form for containers is 'Dewdrop' (10cm/4in), which has blue-grey foliage and sweetly scented, fringed white flowers with a green eye. Taller pinks, up to 30cm (12in), include 'Laced Monarch', whose pink flowers are laced with purple, and 'Doris', shrimp-pink with a red eye.

DICENTRA

P ☼ ● ⊟ | SPRING | SUMMER | AUTUMN | WINTER

Known as 'bleeding heart', this has ferny, delicate blue-green foliage and graceful, arching stems of little locket-shaped flowers. *D. spectabilis* has rosy red and white flowers, while the cultivar 'Alba' is pure white. Lovely for arrangements with plants liking similar conditions. Both reach about 60cm (2ft).

ERICA *carnea*

S ☼ ☀ ⊟ | SPRING | SUMMER | AUTUMN | WINTER

These winter-flowering heathers are lime-tolerant, growing 15–30cm (6–12in) tall, usually having dark green foliage, and flowers in white, pink or magenta shades. Some have very attractive long spikes, and they provide colour over a long period. Some good forms include 'Isabell' with white flowers, 'Myretoun Ruby' which is carmine-red, and 'Vivellii', with flowers of deepest red over bronze foliage.

Dianthus 'Nyewoods Cream'

⊟ moisture-retentive   ⊟ ordinary drainage   ⊔ good drainage   ⊔ sharp drainage   ▮ ▮ ▮ flowering season

ERIGERON

| P ☀ ⊔ | SPRING | SUMMER | AUTUMN | WINTER |

Delightful rayed daisy flowers with yellow centres, borne above clumps of low evergreen foliage. 'Charity' is light pink and 'Dignity' violet-blue, both reaching 45cm (18in) and adding colour for a long time over summer. For smaller pots, 'Four Winds' is ideal, growing only to 25cm (10in) with light pinky-mauve blooms.

ERODIUM

| A ☀ ⊔ | SPRING | SUMMER | AUTUMN | WINTER |

Long-flowering, mounded alpines (5cm/2in) for sinks or pans, the small, dark green leaves covered almost continually with rounded flowers veined in deeper colours. *E. reichardii* is white, *E.* x *variabile* 'Bishop's Form' has very bright deep rose pink flowers, and there is a tiny double pink form, 'Flore Pleno'.

ESCALLONIA

| S ☀ ☽ ⊔ | SPRING | SUMMER | AUTUMN | WINTER |

There are some compact forms of this evergreen shrub, with glossy dark green foliage attractive all year, and prolific flowers. 'Red Elf' grows only 1m (3ft 3in) high and has intense crimson-red flowers, while 'Red Dream', although slightly taller, has very dense foliage and plum-red flowers.

EUONYMUS

| S ☀ ☽ ⊔ | SPRING | SUMMER | AUTUMN | WINTER |

These are adaptable shrubs, tolerant of most conditions, the evergreen forms being valuable for their variegated or coloured foliage, and the deciduous ones for brilliant autumn colour. They have insignificant flowers, but brightly coloured lobed fruits in autumn. Any of the smaller types are excellent for container arrangements. *E. alatus* 'Compactus' is like a miniature spindleberry, dense and slow-growing, reliably colouring well in autumn. The leaves turn brilliant crimson-pink while the reddish lobed fruits split open to reveal bright orange-coated seeds inside. *E. fortunei* has many named forms, with leathery evergreen leaves. 'Canadale Gold' grows upright to 45–60cm (18–24in), the large leaves

widely margined yellow. 'Golden Pillar' is shorter and more compact, to 30cm (12in), with dark green and gold foliage. 'Emerald Gaiety', with green and white variegated leaves, and 'Emerald 'n' Gold', with striking golden variegated foliage, form spreading hummocks, or can trail through other plants. 'Minimus' is a ground-hugging form with tiny green leaves on long stems which can also trail or hang, and is useful for underplanting. All evergreen forms respond well to pruning to keep them more compact if necessary, and fresh young growth is particularly attractive.

EUPHORBIA

| P ☀ ☽ ⊔ | SPRING | SUMMER | AUTUMN | WINTER |

The spurges make decorative additions to containers, as many have attractively coloured foliage as well as flowers. Their milky-white sap may irritate skin or eyes, so take care when handling. *E. griffithii* 'Fireglow' (60cm/12in) has brilliant flame-coloured heads of flowers, and *E. amygdaloides* 'Rubra' (45cm/18in) has beetroot-red new growths, dark leaves on maroon stems and bright yellow-green flowers. *E. myrsinites* (15cm/6in) is lovely in a low pan, with its trailing stems clothed in blue-grey fleshy leaves and ending in lime-green flower heads.

FORSYTHIA

| S ☀ ☽ ⊔ | SPRING | SUMMER | AUTUMN | WINTER |

Deciduous shrubs flowering in early spring, extremely floriferous, the leaves emerging after the flowers. Cut back flowering shoots to within a few centimetres of old wood after flowering. *F.* 'Paulina' is slow-growing, with a dwarf habit to 40cm (16in) and golden-yellow flowers. *F.* x *intermedia* 'Minigold' is compact and upright, with deep yellow flowers.

FRANKENIA *thymifolia*

| A ☀ ⊔ | SPRING | SUMMER | AUTUMN | WINTER |

An excellent small plant for sinks and pans, or for trailing over edges of pots, this has grey-green mats of tiny foliage, tinted with red, and clusters of pink stemless flowers.

A = alpine   B = bulb   P = perennial   S = shrub   ☀ sun   ☽ semi-shade   ● shade

FUCHSIA

S ☀ ◐ ⊔ | SPRING | SUMMER | AUTUMN | WINTER

Hardy fuchsias are good container plants, providing colour for months at a time, late in the year. Plant them deeply and cut old stems back in late spring to allow fresh new growth from the base. 'Mrs Popple' is reliable, growing up to 80cm (32in), and is very bushy. The large, plump flowers have carmine sepals and a deep violet corolla. 'Genii' has yellow foliage with cerise and violet flowers, while 'Margaret', which is taller at 1.5m (5ft), has large flowers with carmine sepals and a frilly purple corolla.

GALANTHUS

B ◐ ⊟ | SPRING | SUMMER | AUTUMN | WINTER

Snowdrops epitomize the beginning of spring, and look wonderful under deciduous shrubs in containers or among perennials. *G. nivalis* is the single snowdrop, with dainty hanging white heads, and 'Flore Pleno' is very easy to grow, with fully double white flowers marked green. There are many special named forms you may like to try as well, but these two spread very readily and will give an increasingly good show every year.

GAULTHERIA *procumbens*

S ● ◐ ⊟ | SPRING | SUMMER | AUTUMN | WINTER

A carpeting dwarf shrub 10cm (4in) high with a greater spread, lovely in low, wide pans or bowls. It has dark glossy green, evergreen foliage and white urn-shaped flowers followed by bright red berries, so it is particularly attractive in autumn and winter. It must have lime-free, peaty soil and be kept moist.

GERANIUM

P ☀ ● ⊟ | SPRING | SUMMER | AUTUMN | WINTER

There are so many hardy geraniums to choose from, suitable for all sizes of container and just about any situation. They have very long flowering periods,

Geranium sanguineum **var.** *striatum*

⊞ moisture-retentive   ⊟ ordinary drainage   ⊔ good drainage   ⊔ sharp drainage | | | | | flowering season

Hebe 'Primley Gem'

mounds of dense foliage, and their long flowering stems will intertwine and ramble through other plants. A small selection is mentioned here to give some idea of their variety. *G. nodosum* (30cm/12in) has thin stems of lilac, crimson-veined flowers, while *G. phaeum* (75cm/2ft 6in) carries sombre maroon reflexed flowers, or white ones in its form 'Album'. These three are particularly good for shady positions. *G. pratense* 'Mrs Kendall Clarke' (60cm/2ft) is pale blue, *G. pratense* 'Plenum Violaceum' (60cm/2ft) is very showy with double purple flowers, and *G.* x *riversleaianum* 'Russell Prichard' (20cm/8in) has bright magenta flowers over greyish-green leaves. *G. wallichianum* 'Buxton's Variety' (30cm/12in) has a scrambling growth habit, and its lax stems will trail beautifully, with blue, white-eyed flowers borne over a very long period. *G. sanguineum* var. *striatum* (15cm/6in) is a smaller type for edging pots or adding to alpine hanging baskets. It has masses of clear pink blooms, and there is a white form, 'Album'. An excellent small one for sinks is *G. dalmaticum* (10cm/4in), which has glossy green leaves taking on rich autumn tints, and pretty pink flowers.

GYPSOPHILA *repens*

A ☀ ⊔		SPRING	SUMMER	AUTUMN	WINTER

The trailing alpine gypsophilas are invaluable for edging containers, associating well with other alpines, dwarf shrubs and patio roses. All have prostrate stems clothed in neat blue-green or grey-green leaves, carrying many sprays of little round flowers. 'Dubia' and 'Rosea' are soft pink, and there is also a white-flowered form.

A = alpine   B = bulb   P = perennial   S = shrub   ☀ sun   ☀ semi-shade   ● shade

HEBE

| S | ☀ | ▣ | SPRING | SUMMER | AUTUMN | WINTER |

Dwarf hebes make excellent container plants, as they are evergreen, often have good foliage colour, and produce white, mauve or pink spikes of flowers. Some flower for a few weeks, others over a long season. Some have attractive purple-flushed foliage over winter. 'Autumn Glory' (60–80cm/2ft–2ft 8in) has red-edged leaves and dark violet flowers in late summer and autumn, while 'Nicola's Blush' (40cm/16in) carries beautiful pink flower spikes which fade to white, giving a two-tone effect, and is long-flowering until late autumn. 'Primley Gem' (60cm/2ft) has wavy-edged foliage with red margins, and purple blooms fading to lilac in summer. These are lovely bushy forms for medium to large containers. A smaller species is *H. recurva* (30cm/12in), with elegant, narrow grey leaves and masses of white flowers in late summer. *H. ochracea* 'James Stirling' (40cm/16in) is completely different, forming a densely branched low shrub of a wonderful old-gold colour, the tiny scale-like leaves glowing particularly brightly in winter. *H. pinguifolia* 'Pagei' (15cm/6in) forms carpeting mounds of grey leaves with white flowers in late spring, and is ideal for edging containers or for small pots. Two tiny forms for sinks are *H.* 'Colwall' (5cm/2in), a prostrate mat with mauve flowers, and 'Jasper' (15–20cm/6–8in), a fresh green bun bearing white flowers.

HEDERA *helix*

| S | ☀ | ● | ▣ | SPRING | SUMMER | AUTUMN | WINTER |

Ivies are useful for trailing over the sides of a pot, and can form dense ground cover under deciduous shrubs, contributing foliage when the shrub is bare. There are many with attractively variegated, splashed and speckled leaves, some with exaggerated points, others with frilled or crimped margins, or puckered leaves. Choose one to harmonize with your colour scheme, or use a plain green one such as 'Green Feather' if you are already using several coloured plants. 'Spetchley' is a slow-growing miniature with tiny dark green leaves clustered on the stems, suitable for small plantings or for sinks.

HELIANTHEMUM

| A | ☀ | ▣ | SPRING | SUMMER | AUTUMN | WINTER |

Rock roses give a real splash of colour all summer with their bright or pastel flowers, and they relish dry, hot conditions. There are many named forms, with green or grey foliage, single or double flowers. Some recommended ones include 'Ben Ledi' with deep rose-red flowers, 'Sterntaler' with large golden-yellow blooms, 'Wisley White' with pure white flowers, 'Sudbury Gem' with deep pink flowers and 'Wisley Primrose' with soft primrose-yellow flowers. All are 15–20cm high (6–8in). A smaller one for a sink is *H. lunulatum*, whose prostrate stems of grey leaves bear small but showy yellow flowers.

HELLEBORUS

| P | ● | ☀ | ▣ | SPRING | SUMMER | AUTUMN | WINTER |

These handsome perennials, with their attractive, deeply fingered foliage and saucer-shaped flowers over the cold months, are good companions for other perennials which like shady conditions and moist, rich compost. The Christmas rose, *H. niger* (30cm/12in),

Hedera helix 'Spetchley'

▣ moisture-retentive   ▣ ordinary drainage   ▣ good drainage   ▢ sharp drainage   ▭ flowering season has nodding white blooms even in early winter. The Lenten rose, *H. orientalis* (30–40cm/12–16in), produces nodding flowers of various colours from late winter to mid-spring. Hybrids can be found with white, pink, plum or maroon flowers, sometimes spotted inside with crimson or maroon. New forms are now available with yellow, green or almost black flowers, often beautifully marked. *H.* x *sternii* (45cm/18in) has clusters of pinkish-green flowers in spring, above marbled foliage.

HEUCHERA

| P ☼ ▣ | SPRING | SUMMER | AUTUMN | WINTER |

You will find an increasing range of these perennials, with their overlapping rounded leaves, sometimes puckered and often having irregular edges. They are excellent for providing foliage shape and colour. Wiry stems, 30–45cm (12–18in) high, carry dainty heads of many tiny flowers. *H. micrantha* var. *diversifolia* 'Palace Purple' is well known, forming mounds of dark bronze-red leaves, paler beneath, with clouds of tiny white flowers. *H.* 'Pewter Moon' has silvery-grey and purple leaves, maroon beneath, and ice-pink flowers. Others have almost self-explanatory names, such as 'Chocolate Ruffles' and 'Strawberry Swirl'. A neat little one for smaller plantings is *H. pulchella*, its low green mounds topped by 12cm (5in) stems of pink flowers.

HOSTA

| P ● ☼ ▣ | SPRING | SUMMER | AUTUMN | WINTER |

Handsome clumps of broad foliage, often heavily corrugated, sometimes with undulating margins, and either green, blue or variegated. Heads of mauve or white flowers are borne on sturdy stems. Excellent for pots in shady positions in moist compost. 'Halcyon' (40cm/16in) has tapering leaves of bright silvery-grey, appearing blue, and heavy clusters of lilac flowers. The large leaves of *H. fortunei* var. *albopicta* (60cm/2ft) unfurl creamy-yellow with a green margin, becoming soft green in summer. *H.* 'Yellow Splash' is smaller at 30cm (12in), with bright variegated leaves of green, edged white and yellow.

HOUTTUYNIA *cordata* 'Chameleon'

| P ☼ ▣ | SPRING | SUMMER | AUTUMN | WINTER |

A colourful plant for late spring to autumn, with heart-shaped green leaves splashed yellow and red, and small white flowers, growing to 15cm (6in). It makes a good individual container plant, or can be grown with other moisture-loving plants in partial shade. Excellent for brightening up a scheme.

HYDRANGEA *paniculata*

| S ☼ ▣ | SPRING | SUMMER | AUTUMN | WINTER |

A lovely deciduous shrub for late flowering, the compact form 'Kyushu' reaches up to 2m (6ft 6in), but can be kept shorter in a container. Creamy-white flowers are carried in tapering cone-shaped heads, with tiny flowers surrounded by more showy sterile ones with their large petal-like sepals.

HYPERICUM

| A ☼ ▃ | SPRING | SUMMER | AUTUMN | WINTER |

The small alpine forms are colourful additions to sinks, pans and small pots. The shrubby *H. olympicum* (20cm/8in) bears glaucous foliage and large golden-yellow flowers with prominent stamens over a long period in summer. *H. reptans* (3cm/1¼in) has slender trailing stems clothed in bronze, red-tinged leaves ending in round rich golden flowers, forming a leafy sheet down the side of the sink.

IBERIS

| P ☼ ▃ | SPRING | SUMMER | AUTUMN | WINTER |

Candytuft, with its shrubby evergreen foliage and mass of early summer flowers, is an invaluable plant to use for edging or trailing in a container. *I. sempervirens* 'Schneeflocke' (25cm/10in) produces pure white flowers massed above dark green mats.

IRIS

| P ☼ ▃ | SPRING | SUMMER | AUTUMN | WINTER |

Iris pallida 'Variegata' has handsome leaves boldly striped blue-green and primrose yellow, with scented pale mauve flowers. Reaching 60cm (2ft), it can

---

A = alpine   B = bulb   P = perennial   S = shrub   ☼ sun   ☼ semi-shade   ● shade

provide a distinctive foliage contrast. Dwarf bearded irises, usually 20–35cm (8–14in) high, are available in a huge range of colours, the standards and falls (or beards) of the flowers often in different colours and with varying shading or markings. *I.* 'Brighteyes' has soft lemon-yellow standards with brownish-purple spots, and falls flushed blue and green. 'Green Spot' is pure white marked with a green spot, 'Blue Denim' is a mid-blue shade, and 'Prince' is a smoky olive-brown with blue falls. These add subtle colours to a scheme, as well as a contrast in leaf shape.

LAMIUM *maculatum*

| P | ☀ | ● | ▣ | SPRING | SUMMER | AUTUMN | WINTER |

Useful foliage ground cover, for mixed perennial plantings and for edging or underplanting, also producing short spikes of flowers on 10cm (4in) stems. 'White Nancy' has silver-grey leaves and white flowers, 'Beacon Silver' is silvery-white with pink flowers, while 'Pink Pewter' has totally silvered leaves with a crinkly green edge, and pale pink flowers.

LAVANDULA *angustifolia*

| S | ☀ | ⊔ | SPRING | SUMMER | AUTUMN | WINTER |

Lavenders are valuable for fragrance, a long flowering period, and their silvery-grey or silvery-green foliage. Thriving in hot, dry spots, they are best trimmed after flowering to tidy them up and promote fresh growth from the base. 'Imperial Gem' (45cm/18in) has stunning flower spikes of a very dark purple above silvery bushes, and 'Folgate' (45cm/18in) is a compact silvery-green shrub with dense spikes of mid lavender-blue. Taller forms at 60cm (2ft) are 'Twickel Purple', with broad grey-green leaves and a neat rounded habit, carrying long spikes of purple flowers, and 'Hidcote Pink', with pale pink flowers.

LEWISIA *cotyledon*

| A | ☀ | ⊔ | SPRING | SUMMER | AUTUMN | WINTER |

Large evergreen rosettes of broad, fleshy leaves carrying many heads of rounded flowers on 10–15cm (4–6in) stems in a range of colours: usually pink, orange and

Lilium formosanum var. *pricei*

yellow shades, also white and magenta. Although hardy, they resent winter damp around their succulent rosettes, so outside are best grown on a slope among rocks in sinks. They make an excellent display in large strawberry pots.

LILIUM

| B | ☀ | ⊔ | SPRING | SUMMER | AUTUMN | WINTER |

Some of the best summer-flowering bulbs, these make superb container features, with their graceful habit and elegant flowers in a huge range of sizes and colours. Choose special short forms ideal for pots, or add taller ones to perennial containers, ensuring that they have excellent drainage.

▣ moisture-retentive   ▣ ordinary drainage   ⊔ good drainage   ⊔ sharp drainage   ▮ ▮ ▮ ▮ flowering season

Origanum vulgare 'Aureum Crispum'

LYSIMACHIA

| P ☀ ◐ ▣ | Spring | Summer | Autumn | Winter |

L. nummularia 'Aurea', the golden 'creeping Jenny', adds a bright splash as a trailing plant or as ground cover, with long stems clothed in bright gold foliage and deep golden flowers.

MAHONIA *aquifolium*

| S ● ◐ ▣ | Spring | Summer | Autumn | Winter |

Evergreen shrubs with glossy dark green toothed leaves, growing up to 60cm (2ft) and carrying dense clusters of bright yellow flowers in spring. 'Smaragd' has bronzed young leaves, becoming deep green, and 'Apollo' has deep gold flowers.

MELISSA *officinalis*

| P ◐ ▣ | Spring | Summer | Autumn | Winter |

The herb lemon balm (30cm/12in), with strongly veined lemon-scented oval leaves and small pale flowers, adds a bright touch. 'Aurea' has rich yellow leaves, which will scorch in full sun, and 'Variegata' has green leaves splashed yellow.

MENTHA *requienii*

| A ● ◐ ▣ | Spring | Summer | Autumn | Winter |

A tiny mint forming fresh green carpets of rounded leaves, strongly peppermint-scented, studded with microscopic stemless lavender flowers. A good plant for a low pan or for use in sink landscapes.

MINUARTIA

| A ☀ ▣ | Spring | Summer | Autumn | Winter |

Cushion alpines ideal for sinks and pans. *M. circassica* has very fine grassy leaves with loose clusters of white flowers on 10cm (4in) stems. *M. stellata* forms tight, hard cushions of densely packed, bright green foliage, and has almost stemless white flowers.

MYRTUS

| S ☀ ▣ | Spring | Summer | Autumn | Winter |

A compact form of myrtle is *M. communis* subsp. *tarentina*, a pretty evergreen shrub with glossy green, pointed leaves. It is free-flowering, the fragrant pink-tinged white flowers with their fluffy stamens being followed by white berries. It is remarkably hardy, though benefiting from a sheltered spot in cold localities. Reaching 30–45cm (12–18in), it makes a superb container plant.

NANDINA *domestica*

| S ☀ ▣ | Spring | Summer | Autumn | Winter |

The dwarf form 'Firepower', reaching 30–45cm (12–18in), is a semi-evergreen bamboo-like shrub, and an excellent plant for containers in a sheltered spot. It has exciting foliage, the young yellow-green leaves turning a burnished orange-red and pink in autumn, this colour being retained through the winter. Small

---

A = alpine   B = bulb   P = perennial   S = shrub   ☀ sun   ◐ semi-shade   ● shade

white flowers are borne, but it needs a very hot summer to produce its red berries.

NARCISSUS

| B ☼ ☀ ⊔ | SPRING | SUMMER | AUTUMN | WINTER |

There is a huge range of narcissi available, from tiny species for sinks to dwarf forms for little pots or pans and taller varieties for larger containers. They all give a cheering spring display, whether planted in pots on their own, with other bulbs, or with different plants.

NEPETA

| P ☼ ⊔ | SPRING | SUMMER | AUTUMN | WINTER |

The catmints are excellent in sunny, well-drained containers or hanging baskets, flowering all summer and harmonizing with any pastel colour scheme. *N.* x *faassenii* is low-growing, up to 30cm (12in), with scented grey foliage and carrying lavender-blue tubular flowers in loose spikes.

OPHIOPOGON

| P ☼ ● ▣ | SPRING | SUMMER | AUTUMN | WINTER |

These form 15–20cm (6–8in) tufts of arching grassy leaves which provide useful foliage contrast. *O. planiscapus* 'Nigrescens' has very dark, almost black leaves and dense sprays of cream flowers followed by shiny purple-black berries. *O. planiscapus* 'Little Tabby' has arching green leaves with distinctive white margins, and glossy blue-black berries.

ORIGANUM *vulgare*

| P ☼ ⊔ | SPRING | SUMMER | AUTUMN | WINTER |

There are various named forms of marjoram, with scented foliage and white or pink flowers beloved by bees. The coloured-foliage forms are especially attractive for containers; the low mounds of foliage are topped with 20–30cm (8–12in) stems of flowers in summer. 'Aureum Crispum' is a golden marjoram with rounded, crinkled leaves, forming a compact mound, and 'Gold Tip' has pointed green leaves splashed gold. 'Aureum' has totally gold leaves that will scorch in hot sun. 'Polyphant' has charming cream and green foliage.

OSMANTHUS

| S ☼ ⊔ | SPRING | SUMMER | AUTUMN | WINTER |

Attractive evergreen shrubs with dense foliage and fragrant white flowers, borne in spring or autumn depending on the variety. *O. delavayi* is slow-growing up to 90cm (3ft), with small leathery leaves and masses of sweetly scented white flowers in mid-spring. It can be kept compact by regular pruning after flowering.

PARAHEBE

| A ☼ ☀ ⊔ | SPRING | SUMMER | AUTUMN | WINTER |

Reliable, long-flowering little evergreen bushes up to 15cm (6in) high, with leathery, toothed leaves and sprays of delicate flowers for much of the year. *P. catarractae* 'Delight' has lilac-blue, crimson-veined flowers, while 'Rosea' is lower-growing with pink flowers, veined crimson; there is also a white-flowered form. *P. lyallii* is a low-growing spreading plant with masses of white flowers, veined pink, borne over mounds of thick, leathery leaves.

PHLOX *douglasii*

| A ☼ ⊔ | SPRING | SUMMER | AUTUMN | WINTER |

The alpine phloxes form compact tufted cushions (5 x 15cm (2 x 6in) spread) of needle-like green leaves, which become hidden under the colourful flowers produced in late spring. They are excellent for sinks and pans, and can be found in a wide range of colours.

White form of *Parahebe catarractae*

▣ moisture-retentive   ▣ ordinary drainage   ⊔ good drainage   ⊔ sharp drainage | | | | flowering season

'Crackerjack' has brilliant crimson-red flowers, 'Iceberg' has cool, pale ice-blue flowers, and 'Rosea' is smothered in pale pink blooms.

PHORMIUM

| S | ☀ | ㄴ | | SPRING | SUMMER | AUTUMN | WINTER |

The New Zealand flax is extremely architectural, with its imposing sword-like leaves. They are evergreen, and the crowns are best protected during harsh winters. There are several forms with wonderfully colourful leaves. 'Bronze Baby' is a quite dwarf form, to 60cm (2ft), with glossy coppery-red leaves. 'Maori Maiden' has rich, rosy salmon-pink leaves, striped with coral and drooping at the tips, while 'Jester' has lime-green leaves with a pink centre. Both of these are about 1m (3ft 3in) tall, as is 'Sundowner', with wide leaves of greyish-purple edged with creamy-pink bands.

POTENTILLA *fruticosa*

| S | ☀ | ◐ | ㄴ | | SPRING | SUMMER | AUTUMN | WINTER |

Shrubby deciduous plants with a dense twiggy habit, their small leaves and long flowering season making a valuable contribution to container plantings. There are several varieties only 45cm–1m (1ft 6in–3ft 3in) high, so choose one to fit in with the scale of your container. 'Manchu' and 'Abbotswood' are white-flowered, and 'Goldfinger' has brilliant yellow flowers. *Potentilla* 'Sungold' is a particularly neat, compact dwarf form with golden flowers.

PRIMULA

| P | ● | ◐ | ㅌ | | SPRING | SUMMER | AUTUMN | WINTER |

Invaluable plants for adding spring flowers to collections, these are available in many different forms and colours. Pans and pots of brightly coloured primroses can be found anywhere in early spring, and add a cheerful note during dull weather. The 'Wanda' hybrids have a good range of more natural flower shades and flower prolifically, sometimes having bronzed foliage as well. *P.* 'Garryard Guinevere' (15cm/6in) is valuable for its bronze-purple leaves and masses of lilac pink, yellow-eyed flowers. The double

primroses (15cm/6in) are beautiful, thriving in containers with rich compost in a cool position. *P.* 'Alan Robb' is a rich apricot, 'Dawn Ansell' a pure white, and 'Miss Indigo' rich blue, flecked silver. These should be split up every other year and replanted to keep in good condition (put a portion back in the container, and the rest in the garden or in more pots). Named varieties of *P.* x *pubescens* (10cm/4in) resemble miniature auriculas, with many heads of flowers in various colours, and are invaluable for sink plantings. 'Boothman's Variety' is bright crimson and 'Bewerley White' a lovely creamy colour.

PRUNUS

| S | ☀ | ◐ | ㄴ | | SPRING | SUMMER | AUTUMN | WINTER |

Dwarf forms of *Prunus* are very attractive in pots, and one of the best is *P. incisa* 'Kojo-no-mai', a small shrubby tree up to 1.2m (4ft). It forms a framework of zigzag twigs, clothed in toothed leaves that take on colourful red and orange autumn tints before falling. In early spring it is smothered with pretty pink-tinged pendent flowers before the new leaves emerge.

Prunus incisa 'Kojo-no-mai'

A = alpine   B = bulb   P = perennial   S = shrub   ☀ sun   ◐ semi-shade   ● shade

PULMONARIA

| P | ☀ | ⊟ | SPRING | SUMMER | AUTUMN | WINTER |

The lungworts are valuable for their variety of bold, textured, spotted and marbled leaves, together with their early flowering season. *P. saccharata* 'Argentea' has frosted silver leaves, while 'Reginald Kaye' has both large and small silver spots over the leaf surface. *P. longifolia* has long, narrow leaves of dark green with white spots, and rich blue flowers. These pulmonarias are low-growing (20–30cm/8–12in), spreading to 30–45cm (12–18in).

RANUNCULUS *ficaria*

| P | ☼ | ☀ | ⊟ | SPRING | SUMMER | AUTUMN | WINTER |

There are some very ornamental forms of the lesser celandine, 5–8cm (2–3in) in height and spreading to 20cm (8in). 'Brazen Hussy' has wonderful glistening bronze foliage emerging in spring, forming low carpets, followed soon after by shiny golden cup-shaped flowers that open wide in the sunshine. It is a brilliant plant for a colourful, exciting spring display, either alone or with plants that will take over when it becomes dormant in summer. 'Collarette' has flowers like little pompons, bright yellow with a green centre.

RHODODENDRON

| S | ☼ | ☀ | ⊟ | SPRING | SUMMER | AUTUMN | WINTER |

The tiny species *R. impeditum,* 30cm (12in) high, can be grown in an ericaceous sink planting or in a small pan. It makes a neat, domed bush with very close, tiny grey-green leaves, and bears clusters of small starry blue flowers. 'Harry White's Purple' is a very compact form of this with bright purple flowers. The best dwarf rhododendron, ideal for a large pot or tub, is *R. yakushimanum*, forming a domed, compact bush slowly growing up to 1m (3ft 3in). The long, glossy green leaves are covered in brown tomentum (downy hairs) beneath, so it looks attractive all year. It is very free-flowering with round ball-like trusses of flowers, the pink buds opening blush-pink and then becoming white. There are many hybrids available in different colours, but none as compact. Rhododendrons require

Rosa 'Pretty Polly' (patio rose)

ericaceous compost, enriched with peat or leaf-mould. Use rainwater to water with when possible.

ROSA (patio roses)

| S | ☼ | ⊟ | SPRING | SUMMER | AUTUMN | WINTER |

The small stature and tiny blooms of patio roses make them perfect for pots and troughs. They can be found in many colours, and will thrive in good, well-drained compost in a sunny spot. Prune only by removing spent flowers and any damaged or dead wood. They are wonderful underplanted with *Gypsophila repens*, *Thymus* or small *Geranium*. 'Pretty Polly' has soft pink double blooms, 'Little Bo-peep' is a very pale pink, and 'Sweet Dream' has double apricot flowers. These all reach about 45cm (18in).

ROSMARINUS *officinalis*

| S | ☼ | ⊔ | SPRING | SUMMER | AUTUMN | WINTER |

An evergreen aromatic shrub, also used as a culinary herb. The narrow, dark leaves are white beneath, and pale blue flowers are borne all along the stems. Rosemary does well in pots, growing to 60–90cm (2–3ft), and can be clipped or trained into spheres or standards if you wish. Deeper blue forms include

---

⊟ moisture-retentive   ⊡ ordinary drainage   ⊔ good drainage   ⊔ sharp drainage | | | | flowering season

Salvia officinalis 'Icterina'

'Sissinghurst Blue' and 'Benenden Blue', and there is also a more compact, slow-growing white variety, *albiflorus*, with a much tighter growth habit.

SALIX

| S | ☼ | ● | ▣ | | SPRING | SUMMER | AUTUMN | WINTER |

There are some tiny dwarf willows suitable for sinks, and they can add real character to a sink planting. *S. serpyllifolia* is a completely prostrate species with thin stems clothed in tiny bright green leaves, moulding itself closely to any rocks or over the sides of the sink. *S. herbacea* has branching stems of glossy dark green leaves with prominent veining, forming a mat, and catkins in summer. *S. myrsinites* var. *jacquiniana* is a miniature with little shiny green leaves and minute deep red catkins in late spring and early summer. If you want one to resemble a miniature gnarled tree, plant *S.* 'Boydii', an erect willow with thick branches and puckered, deeply textured blue-grey leaves. Although it can reach 45cm (18in), it is extremely slow and will take many years to do so.

SALVIA

| P | ☼ | ◡ | | SPRING | SUMMER | AUTUMN | WINTER |

The sages include forms grown chiefly for their coloured foliage as well as those with attractive flower spikes. *S. officinalis* is culinary sage, and 'Purpurascens' has soft mauve foliage, particularly lovely when new

growth is starting in late spring. 'Tricolor' has cream, pink and purple leaves, while 'Icterina' is soft green and creamy-yellow. All are aromatic. The dense violet-blue spikes of *S. nemorosa* 'Ostfriesland' are attractive in many different schemes, as are the midnight-blue flowers of *S.* x *sylvestris* 'Mainacht', which is early and long-flowering. For a lighter blue colour, choose *S.* x *sylvestris* 'Blauhügel'. All these salvias reach about 45cm (18in).

SANTOLINA

| S | ☼ | ◡ | | SPRING | SUMMER | AUTUMN | WINTER |

The cotton lavenders have evergreen threadlike green or silver foliage, strongly aromatic, and little button flowers of bright or primrose yellow. They respond well to clipping, and need to be cut down hard in mid-spring to promote the new growth from the base in order to keep them tidy. You can remove the flowers if you want to grow them as silver foliage plants. 'Lambrook Silver' (30cm/12in) has close, compact growth of intense silver leaves, and *S. rosmarinifolia* subsp. *rosmarinifolia* 'Primrose Gem' (45cm/18in) has emerald-green foliage and soft yellow flowers. *S. chamaecyparissus* 'Small-Ness' (15cm/6in) is a delightful miniature of silvery green, ideal for a sink or for making miniature knot garden hedges.

Saponaria ocymoides

A = alpine   B = bulb   P = perennial   S = shrub   ☼ sun   ◐ semi-shade   ● shade

Saxifraga burseriana 'Prince Hal'

SAPONARIA *ocymoides*

| A | ☼ | ⊔ | SPRING | SUMMER | AUTUMN | WINTER |

The leafy, trailing 20cm (8in) stems of Tumbling Ted can form a carpet or a cascading mat, and are covered in bright pink flowers giving a wonderful display of colour. There is a white form 'Snow Tip', equally floriferous, and both of these are good trailing plants for containers.

SAXIFRAGA

| A | ◐ | ⊔ | SPRING | SUMMER | AUTUMN | WINTER |

Early-flowering saxifrages have tight rosettes of leaves and flowers in many colours, often by late winter, and are 5–7cm (2–3in) high. *S.* x *anglica* 'Cranbourne' is blue-grey with stemless pink flowers, *S.* x *anglica* 'Grace Farwell' is dark green with rich wine-red flowers, and *S.* x *kellereri* 'Kewensis' has very pale pink flowers borne on red stems above silver cushions. *S.* x *elisabethae* 'Primrose Dame' is a reliable yellow with hard green rosettes, *S.* x *boydilacina* 'Penelope' has greyish-green leaves and pale peachy-pink flowers, and *S. burseriana* 'Prince Hal' has large white blooms on salmon-pink stems. *S.* x *hardingii* 'Iris Prichard' is a distinctive, very early-flowering one with silver-encrusted rosettes and buff-apricot flowers.

The silver saxifrages have encrusted rosettes and often have spoon-shaped leaves; many sprays of dainty flowers on 10–20cm (4–8in) stems are carried in late spring and early summer. *S.* x *burnatii* 'Esther' has creamy-yellow flowers on long horizontal stems, and *S.* 'Doctor Ramsey' has handsome silvered rosettes with white flowers.

⊟ moisture-retentive   ⊟ ordinary drainage   ⊔ good drainage   ⊔ sharp drainage | | | | flowering season

Other types include 'Winifred Bevington' (15cm/ 6in), with tidy green rosettes and sprays of white, pink-spotted flowers in summer. All these are suitable for sinks and pans, as collections or with other alpines.

The larger London pride, *S.* x *urbium* (25cm/10in), bears masses of dainty, starry white flowers spotted red over dense rosettes, and associates well in containers with small perennials which like similar conditions.

SCLERANTHUS *biflorus*

| A ☼ ⊔ | SPRING | SUMMER | AUTUMN | WINTER |

A dense, compact cushion-forming plant with minute needle-like leaves and tiny flowers in pairs, which will mound itself over rocks and even form irregular hummocks within itself. It is ideal for creating 'grassy' areas in miniature landscapes, or for growing in a wide, low pan. *S. uniflorus* is very similar, but with solitary flowers.

SEDUM

| A/P ☼ ⊔ | SPRING | SUMMER | AUTUMN | WINTER |

A huge range of alpines and perennials with thick, fleshy leaves and large heads of many starry flowers in late summer. Trailing types are lovely for edging pots and in hanging baskets. *S. kamtschaticum* var. *floriferum* 'Weihenstephaner Gold' has dark green, leafy 15cm (6in) stems carrying heads of golden starry

Sedum kamtschaticum var. *floriferum* 'Weihenstephaner Gold'

Sempervivum 'Corsair'

flowers, turning reddish with age. *S. spurium* var. *album* has pale green foliage and pure white heads, while *S. spurium* 'Variegatum' carries pale pink flowers and has colourful pink, cream and grey leaves. *S.* 'Ruby Glow' has long, lax, radiating 25cm (10in) stems of green, purple-tinged succulent leaves, ending in deep rose-pink flowers. A neat form suitable for a sink is *S. spathulifolium* 'Cape Blanco', with rosettes of rounded leaves covered in a thick white bloom, and heads of yellow flowers on 5cm (2in) stems. A short, compact upright form for containers is *S. spectabile* 'Brilliant' (30cm/12in), with large, flat bright pink flower heads over pale green fleshy leaves.

SEMPERVIVUM

| A ☼ ⊔ | SPRING | SUMMER | AUTUMN | WINTER |

Succulent alpines with neat rosettes of leaves showing a wide range of subtle and bright colours, including deep red, soft mauve and lime green. Sometimes leaves are tipped dark red, or show colour changes during the year, the richest and deepest colours usually showing in summer. Others have fine cobwebbing on the rosettes. Rosette size varies considerably, from tiny, tight ones to large, imposing types. Reddish-brown, rose or

---

A = alpine   B = bulb   P = perennial   S = shrub   ☼ sun   ☼ semi-shade   ● shade

yellow flowers are borne in summer, and although the main flowering rosette dies, numerous offsets are produced. There are thousands of named forms to choose from, and they all thrive in well-drained, gritty compost in full sun. They are ideal for pans and troughs, grown singly or in mixed groups of different colours.

SILENE *acaulis*

| A ☼ ⊔ | SPRING | SUMMER | AUTUMN | WINTER |

A cushion alpine for sinks, forming mats of thin, bright green leaves and small pink flowers. An even smaller form is 'Mount Snowdon', a very tight cushion with minute pink flowers.

SISYRINCHIUM

| A/P ☼ ⊔ | SPRING | SUMMER | AUTUMN | WINTER |

These have iris-like leaves and starry flowers opening in the sun. *S. striatum* reaches 60cm (2ft), with linear leaves giving contrast in plantings, and many slender spires of pale yellow flowers. The leaves of the named form 'Aunt May' are boldly striped with creamy-yellow, associating well with blue-flowered plants. This grows to 45cm (18in) high. *S. idahoense* is a neat little species 10cm (4in) in height, ideal for sinks and small pots, with compact tufts of leaves and deep blue-purple flowers. There is an equally lovely pure white form, *S. idahoense* 'Album'.

Sisyrinchium idahoense

🔳 moisture-retentive   🔲 ordinary drainage   ⊔ good drainage   ⊔ sharp drainage   ▮ ▮ ▮ ▮ flowering season

Thymus x *citriodorus* 'Archer's Gold'

SPIRAEA *japonica*

| S | ☀ | ◑ | ⊔ | SPRING | SUMMER | AUTUMN | WINTER |

Deciduous shrubs with a number of dwarf forms, including 'Gold Mound' at 25cm (10in) high, with bright golden leaves, and 'Nyewoods' at 30cm (12in) with light green foliage. Both have flattened heads of numerous deep rose-pink flowers. They form compact twiggy bushes and just need spent flowers and old wood pruned out.

STACHYS *byzantina*

| P | ☀ | ⊔ | SPRING | SUMMER | AUTUMN | WINTER |

Bold, silky silver foliage in low carpets gives this plant its nickname of 'lamb's ears'. Mauve flowers in woolly spikes (30cm/12in) appear in summer. There is also a non-flowering form 'Silver Carpet', which is more suitable if you just want the foliage effect. They associate well with other sun-lovers in medium to large containers.

A = alpine   B = bulb   P = perennial   S = shrub   ☀ sun   ◑ semi-shade   ● shade

SYRINGA

| S | ☼ | ⊔ | | SPRING | SUMMER | AUTUMN | WINTER |

The Korean lilac is a lovely dwarf lilac that makes an excellent container specimen. *S. meyeri* var. *spontanea* 'Palibin' is slow-growing to 60–90cm (2–3ft), forming a compact shrub with glossy leaves and heads of sweetly fragrant lilac-pink flowers in profusion.

TANACETUM *densum* subsp. *amani*

| P | ☼ | ⊔ | | SPRING | SUMMER | AUTUMN | WINTER |

A beautiful low mounded foliage plant that has soft, deeply dissected silvery-grey leaves, growing 10–15cm (4–6in) high with a wider spread. It is lovely in a low, wide bowl or mixed with other sun-loving plants.

THYMUS

| A | ☼ | ⊔ | | SPRING | SUMMER | AUTUMN | WINTER |

There are several prostrate or bushy thymes, some with aromatic leaves, some coloured or variegated, all carrying heads of white, mauve or pink flowers beloved by bees. *T.* x *citriodorus* 'Golden Queen' (30cm/12in) is an upright, bushy, lemon-scented form with green leaves edged with gold. 'Archer's Gold' forms a low mound (15cm/6in) of bright golden foliage, while *T.* x *citriodorus* 'Silver Queen' (30cm/12in) is variegated green and silver. *T.* 'Peter Davis' is a low, compact bush of aromatic greyish leaves and pinkish-mauve flowers. Only 10cm (4in) high, it can be clipped for miniature knot gardens. *T. herba-barona* forms a tangled mat or will trail, its thin stems covered in dark green caraway-scented leaves. *T. serpyllum* has many named forms, all prostrate mats with many flowers: 'Russetings' has particularly deep mauve flowers, while 'Elfin' is a tight dome of minute foliage, ideal for sinks.

TULIPA

| B | ☼ | ⊔ | | SPRING | SUMMER | AUTUMN | WINTER |

An impressive array of flower shapes, sizes and colours is available for tulips, and there are species, dwarf types and taller ones to choose from. You can find one suitable for most container plantings in sun, and their elegant flowers add splashes of colour all through the spring.

VERONICA

| P | ☼ | ⊔ | | SPRING | SUMMER | AUTUMN | WINTER |

These perennials form mats of foliage bearing tapering spikes of flowers, and there are many different forms in various sizes. *V. gentianoides* produces graceful 45cm (18in) tall pale blue spikes over broad green glossy mats. *V. spicata* 'Heidekind' (20cm/8in) has deep pink flower spikes, and *V. spicata* subsp. *incana* (30cm/12in) is silvery with deep blue flowers. Some lovely trailing ones for containers include *V. pectinata* with long stems clothed in foliage and short spikes of bright blue flowers, and *V. prostrata* with royal blue flowers. *V. peduncularis* 'Georgia Blue' (15cm/6in) makes hummocks of bronzed leaves carrying rich blue, white-eyed flowers in mid-spring.

VIBURNUM *opulus* 'Nanum'

| S | ☼ | ● | ⊟ | SPRING | SUMMER | AUTUMN | WINTER |

This dwarf guelder rose only reaches 45cm (18in), and makes an effective specimen shrub. The dense twigs carry lobed, maple-like leaves that take on rich red and burgundy shades in autumn. The red twigs are also colourful for winter.

VINCA *minor*

| P | ☼ | ● | ⊟ | SPRING | SUMMER | AUTUMN | WINTER |

The smaller periwinkles are useful in larger containers, for ground cover or trailing down the sides, and they are tolerant of shade. 'Alba Variegata' is especially attractive, with green leaves edged creamy-yellow, and white flowers.

VIOLA

| P | ☼ | ● | ⊟ | SPRING | SUMMER | AUTUMN | WINTER |

Violets are lovely additions to containers, flowering for a long period. There are many different ones to suit all colour schemes, growing to 10–15cm (4–6in). 'Molly Sanderson' has velvety black flowers with a tiny golden eye, borne from spring until autumn. *V. cornuta* 'Alba' is a long-flowering white form, and *V.* 'Moonlight' is a soft creamy-yellow with a yellow eye. 'Milkmaid' has white flowers washed with blue.

⊟ moisture-retentive   ⊟ ordinary drainage   ⊔ good drainage   ⊔ sharp drainage | | | | flowering season

Grasses and sedges

CAREX

☼ ◑ ▣ | SPRING | SUMMER | AUTUMN | WINTER

The sedges have a wide variety of sizes and leaf colours, offering narrow foliage and an arching shape. The bronze form of *C. comans* (25cm/10in) has grassy foliage with the leaves curling at the tips. *C. ornithopoda* 'Variegata' (15cm/6in) makes much smaller tufts, with narrow green and yellow striped leaves. If you want one that stays really bright all year round, use *C. oshimensis* 'Evergold' (20cm/8in) with its low, arching clumps of variegated leaves, green with a golden central band.

FESTUCA

☼ ⊔ | SPRING | SUMMER | AUTUMN | WINTER

These ornamental grasses have very fine foliage and compact flowering spikes on taller stems. The blue species *F. glauca* has many improved named forms, such as 'Elijah Blue' (30–45cm/12–18in), with dense tufts of a brilliant silvery blue, and 'Blaufuchs' (20cm/8in), a smaller, neat tufted grass of bright blue. *F. eskia* (15cm/6in) has brilliant green, extremely fine soft foliage and dainty green flower spikes that turn reddish-brown. A very ornamental grass, with fine blue-green leaves, is *F. amethystina*, bearing attractive drooping spikelets of green and violet.

KOELERIA *vallesiana*

☼ ⊔ | SPRING | SUMMER | AUTUMN | WINTER

This is a very low, dense tuft of narrow grey-green leaves, producing stiff stems of purplish-green flower spikes on 30cm (12in) stems, ideal if you just want a touch of grassy foliage.

PENNISETUM

☼ ⊔ | SPRING | SUMMER | AUTUMN | WINTER

The dwarf fountain grass, *P. alopecuroides* 'Hameln' (60cm/2ft), forms elegant clumps of bright green arching leaves that take on yellow and pinkish-orange tints in autumn, becoming pale brown in winter. Bronzed red, spiky bottlebrush flowers add to its appeal.

STIPA

☼ ⊔ | SPRING | SUMMER | AUTUMN | WINTER

A graceful, attractive grass, reaching 45cm (18in), with very fine light green leaves and feathery plumes of buff flowers that wave in the slightest breeze.

Miniature ferns

ASPLENIUM *trichomanes* 'Incisum'

● ◑ ▣ MOIST, PEATY

A tiny, very slow-growing, dainty form, only 15cm (6in) high, ideal for sinks. Slender fronds bear tiny fresh green pinnae on very dark midribs.

WOODSIA *polystichoides*

◑ ☼ ▣ MOIST, PEATY

A dense, tufted deciduous fern with bright green toothed pinnae. Reaching 15cm (6in) in height, this is another small fern suitable for sinks.

Dwarf and miniature conifers

CHAMAECYPARIS

☼ ◑ ▣

A recommended slow form for sinks or pans is *C. lawsoniana* 'Gnome'. It is a tight, round bun of very dark green, densely branched foliage, reaching 30cm (12in) in 10 years. *C. thyoides* 'Rubicon' is a wonderful addition to a larger container, its compact grey-green foliage turning a rich wine-red in winter. It slowly reaches 60cm (2ft) in 10 years, forming a broad cone shape.

CRYPTOMERIA

☼ ◑ ▣

One of the best forms for sinks is *C. japonica* 'Compressa', a tiny, congested globe of bronzed green foliage, taking on deeper bronze and red tints in winter. It grows very slowly to 20cm (8in) in 10 years.

A = alpine   B = bulb   P = perennial   S = shrub   ☼ sun   ◑ semi-shade   ● shade

Chamaecyparis lawsoniana 'Gnome'

JUNIPERUS

☼ ☽ ⊟

These have somewhat prickly, aromatic foliage. *J. communis* 'Compressa' is ideal for a sink or small pot, forming a column of blue-grey foliage up to 40cm (16in) in 10 years. It forms a good contrast to mounded and prostrate plants. *J. squamata* 'Blue Star' (30 x 45cm/ 12 x 18in) is a very fine dwarf conifer forming a star-like shape of brilliant silvery-blue dense foliage.

PICEA

☼ ☽ ⊟

A wonderful little spruce for containers is the rounded bun *P. mariana* 'Nana' (20cm/8in), with dense blue-grey foliage. This would be slow enough for a large sink as well as an individual pot.

PINUS *mugo*

☼ ☽ ⊟

There are many good named dwarf forms of the mountain pine, growing to about 1m (3ft 3in). They have bushy dark green foliage, the leaves long and needle-like, and the bright green young growth is very attractive in spring. Examples include 'Gnom', 'Humpy' and 'Mops'.

THUJA

☼ ☽ ⊟

T. occidentalis 'Caespitosa' is an excellent miniature conifer for sinks and pans, making a low hummock of irregular flattened foliage, yellowish-green in colour. It will grow to 15 x 30cm (6 x 12in) in 10 years.

⊟ moisture-retentive   ▣ ordinary drainage   ⊔ good drainage   ⊔ sharp drainage   │ │   │   │ flowering season

About the authors

Chris Wheeler has an honours degree in Agriculture, and was involved in training and landscaping, including much tree planting in the aftermath of the Great Storm of 1987, before he and Valerie started their own nursery.

He has considerable experience in growing plants and teaching gardeners at all levels how to get the most out of their gardens. He lectures widely and runs a variety of practical gardening courses, and is chairman of a local training group.

A self-taught photographer, Chris specializes in environmental subjects, contributing to picture libraries and specialist publications.

Valerie Wheeler gained an honours degree in Horticultural Science at Wye College, London University, then worked in research and commercial horticulture.

She has many years' experience in designing and supplying the plants for sinks, containers and raised beds, her postal design service being available nationwide. She writes and produces all the nursery's catalogues and cultural notes, and has written a number of articles for gardening publications. She has also written booklets on sink plants and dwarf hebes for the nursery's customers.

Aside from gardening, Valerie enjoys all forms of embroidery, much of which adorns the walls at home.

Their mail-order nursery, Siskin Plants, specializes in dwarf hardy plants, particularly trough plants, sempervivums and dwarf hebes. Chris and Valerie hold the National Collection of Dwarf Hebes (East Anglia), containing over one hundred species and cultivars.

They enjoy growing all kinds of plants in their own garden, especially in sinks, home-made troughs and containers, as well as several raised beds and borders.

Index

Page numbers in **bold type** indicate photographs

GMC PUBLICATIONS

BOOKS

WOODCARVING

The Art of the Woodcarver	GMC Publications
Carving Architectural Detail in Wood: The Classical Tradition	
	Frederick Wilbur
Carving Birds & Beasts	GMC Publications
Carving the Human Figure: Studies in Wood and Stone	Dick Onians
Carving Nature: Wildlife Studies in Wood	Frank Fox-Wilson
Carving Realistic Birds	David Tippey
Decorative Woodcarving	Jeremy Williams
Elements of Woodcarving	Chris Pye
Essential Woodcarving Techniques	Dick Onians
Further Useful Tips for Woodcarvers	GMC Publications
Lettercarving in Wood: A Practical Course	Chris Pye
Making & Using Working Drawings for Realistic Model Animals	
	Basil F. Fordham
Power Tools for Woodcarving	David Tippey
Practical Tips for Turners & Carvers	GMC Publications
Relief Carving in Wood: A Practical Introduction	Chris Pye
Understanding Woodcarving	GMC Publications
Understanding Woodcarving in the Round	GMC Publications
Useful Techniques for Woodcarvers	GMC Publications
Wildfowl Carving – Volume 1	Jim Pearce
Wildfowl Carving – Volume 2	Jim Pearce
Woodcarving: A Complete Course	Ron Butterfield
Woodcarving: A Foundation Course	Zoë Gertner
Woodcarving for Beginners	GMC Publications
Woodcarving Tools & Equipment Test Reports	GMC Publications
Woodcarving Tools, Materials & Equipment	Chris Pye

WOODTURNING

Adventures in Woodturning	David Springett
Bert Marsh: Woodturner	Bert Marsh
Bowl Turning Techniques Masterclass	Tony Boase
Colouring Techniques for Woodturners	Jan Sanders
Contemporary Turned Wood: New Perspectives in a Rich Tradition	
	Ray Leier, Jan Peters & Kevin Wallace
The Craftsman Woodturner	Peter Child
Decorative Techniques for Woodturners	Hilary Bowen
Fun at the Lathe	R.C. Bell
Illustrated Woodturning Techniques	John Hunnex
Intermediate Woodturning Projects	GMC Publications
Keith Rowley's Woodturning Projects	Keith Rowley
Practical Tips for Turners & Carvers	GMC Publications
Turning Green Wood	Michael O'Donnell
Turning Miniatures in Wood	John Sainsbury
Turning Pens and Pencils	Kip Christensen & Rex Burningham
Understanding Woodturning	Ann & Bob Phillips
Useful Techniques for Woodturners	GMC Publications
Useful Woodturning Projects	GMC Publications
Woodturning: Bowls, Platters, Hollow Forms, Vases, Vessels, Bottles, Flasks, Tankards, Plates	GMC Publications
Woodturning: A Foundation Course (New Edition)	Keith Rowley
Woodturning: A Fresh Approach	Robert Chapman
Woodturning: An Individual Approach	Dave Regester
Woodturning: A Source Book of Shapes	John Hunnex
Woodturning Jewellery	Hilary Bowen
Woodturning Masterclass	Tony Boase
Woodturning Techniques	GMC Publications
Woodturning Tools & Equipment Test Reports	GMC Publications
Woodturning Wizardry	David Springett

WOODWORKING

Advanced Scrollsaw Projects	GMC Publications
Bird Boxes and Feeders for the Garden	Dave Mackenzie
Complete Woodfinishing	Ian Hosker

David Charlesworth's Furniture-Making Techniques	David Charlesworth
The Encyclopedia of Joint Making	Terrie Noll
Furniture & Cabinetmaking Projects	GMC Publications
Furniture-Making Projects for the Wood Craftsman	GMC Publications
Furniture-Making Techniques for the Wood Craftsman	GMC Publications
Furniture Projects	Rod Wales
Furniture Restoration (Practical Crafts)	Kevin Jan Bonner
Furniture Restoration and Repair for Beginners	Kevin Jan Bonner
Furniture Restoration Workshop	Kevin Jan Bonner
Green Woodwork	Mike Abbott
Kevin Ley's Furniture Projects	Kevin Ley
Making & Modifying Woodworking Tools	Jim Kingshott
Making Chairs and Tables	GMC Publications
Making Classic English Furniture	Paul Richardson
Making Little Boxes from Wood	John Bennett
Making Screw Threads in Wood	Fred Holder
Making Shaker Furniture	Barry Jackson
Making Woodwork Aids and Devices	Robert Wearing
Mastering the Router	Ron Fox
Minidrill: Fifteen Projects	John Everett
Pine Furniture Projects for the Home	Dave Mackenzie
Practical Scrollsaw Patterns	John Everett
Router Magic: Jigs, Fixtures and Tricks to Unleash your Router's Full Potential	Bill Hylton
Routing for Beginners	Anthony Bailey
The Scrollsaw: Twenty Projects	John Everett
Sharpening: The Complete Guide	Jim Kingshott
Sharpening Pocket Reference Book	Jim Kingshott
Simple Scrollsaw Projects	GMC Publications
Space-Saving Furniture Projects	Dave Mackenzie
Stickmaking: A Complete Course	Andrew Jones & Clive George
Stickmaking Handbook	Andrew Jones & Clive George
Test Reports: The Router and Furniture & Cabinetmaking	GMC Publications
Veneering: A Complete Course	Ian Hosker
Veneering Handbook	Ian Hosker
Woodfinishing Handbook (Practical Crafts)	Ian Hosker
Woodworking with the Router: Professional Router Techniques any Woodworker can Use	Bill Hylton & Fred Matlack
The Workshop	Jim Kingshott

UPHOLSTERY

The Upholsterer's Pocket Reference Book	David James
Upholstery: A Complete Course (Revised Edition)	David James
Upholstery Restoration	David James
Upholstery Techniques & Projects	David James
Upholstery Tips and Hints	David James

TOYMAKING

Designing & Making Wooden Toys	Terry Kelly
Fun to Make Wooden Toys & Games	Jeff & Jennie Loader
Restoring Rocking Horses	Clive Green & Anthony Dew
Scrollsaw Toy Projects	Ivor Carlyle
Scrollsaw Toys for All Ages	Ivor Carlyle
Wooden Toy Projects	GMC Publications

DOLLS' HOUSES AND MINIATURES

1/12 Scale Character Figures for the Dolls' House	James Carrington
Architecture for Dolls' Houses	Joyce Percival
The Authentic Georgian Dolls' House	Brian Long
A Beginners' Guide to the Dolls' House Hobby	Jean Nisbett
Celtic, Medieval and Tudor Wall Hangings in 1/12 Scale Needlepoint	
	Sandra Whitehead
The Complete Dolls' House Book	Jean Nisbett
The Dolls' House 1/24 Scale: A Complete Introduction	Jean Nisbett
Dolls' House Accessories, Fixtures and Fittings	Andrea Barham

MAGAZINES

WOODTURNING ~ WOODCARVING ~ FURNITURE & CABINETMAKING ~ THE ROUTER
WOODWORKING ~ THE DOLLS' HOUSE MAGAZINE ~ WATER GARDENING
EXOTIC GARDENING ~ GARDEN CALENDAR ~ OUTDOOR PHOTOGRAPHY ~ BUSINESSMATTERS

The above represents a full list of all titles currently published or scheduled to be published.
All are available direct from the Publishers or through bookshops, newsagents and specialist retailers.
To place an order, or to obtain a complete catalogue, contact:

GMC Publications

Castle Place, 166 High Street, Lewes, East Sussex BN7 1XU, United Kingdom
Tel: 01273 488005 Fax: 01273 478606 E-mail: pubs@thegmcgroup.com
Orders by credit card are accepted